We Don't Exactly Get the Welcome Wagon

|We Don't Exactly Get the Welcome Wagon|

*The Experiences of Gay and Lesbian Adolescents
in Child Welfare Systems*

Gerald P. Mallon

Columbia University Press

New York

Columbia University Press
Publishers Since 1893
New York   Chichester, West Sussex

Library of Congress Cataloging-in-Publication Data
Mallon, Gerald P.
    We don't exactly get the Welcome Wagon : the experiences of gay
and lesbian adolescents in child welfare systems / Gerald P. Mallon.
        p.   cm.
    Includes bibliographical references (p.   ) and index.
    ISBN 0-231-10454-5 (cl : acid-free paper). — ISBN 0-231-10455-3
(acid-free paper)
    1. Gay teenagers—Institutional care—North America. 2. Child
welfare—North America. 3. Homophobia—North America. I. Title.
HV1449.M35   1998
362.7'083—dc21
                                                    97-45545
                                                       CIP

Casebound editions of Columbia University Press books are printed on
permanent and durable acid-free paper.
Printed in the United States of America
c 10 9 8 7 6 5 4 3 2 1
p 10 9 8 7 6 5 4 3 2 1

For
Barbara Levy Simon

Contents

Preface

Gay and lesbian history is rooted in decades of hiding and secrecy, when the mere whisper that one was not a stalwart heterosexual could destroy a career or a life. The keepers of public morals sought to keep those who strayed from this position firmly in line. But consequential shifts over time in cultural openness to gays and lesbians have taken place. A trio of events—the groundbreaking work of the late Dr. Evelyn Hooker (1957, 1967), which presented rigorous scientific research to provide indisputable evidence that homosexuality is not a mental illness; the impact of the Stonewall Rebellion of 1969 in New York City, generally regarded as the birth of the gay and lesbian liberation movement; and the elimination of "homosexuality" from the *Diagnostic and Statistical Manual of Mental Disorders* (APA 1974) in 1973—caused society to slowly begin to change its perceptions of homosexuality.

Concurrently, throughout the late 1970s, as social activism in the gay/lesbian communities were nurturing the growth of a new sense of dignity among homosexuals, adult lesbians/gays became increasingly willing to identify themselves openly (Schneider 1991:133). These factors converged to sanction those adolescents who previously would have remained silent to identify themselves openly as gay or lesbian, and to others to express their uncertainty about their own sexual orientation. In light of this ostensible openness, some child welfare practitioners became aware of the existence of gay/lesbian youths on their caseloads, many of whom were involved with social services for reasons other than their sexual orientation.

We Don't Exactly Get the Welcome Wagon explores the lives of fifty-four gay/lesbian young people who, at the time this study was conducted, were living in an out-of-home-care child welfare setting. I have written this book about them because I wanted others to learn about their perspectives and experiences. The central theme of this work focuses on the multiple experiences of the gay/lesbian adolescent within the out-of-home-care setting in which they lived. What emerges from the weaving of themes and constructing of stories culled from extensive tape-recorded interviews in three cities—Los Angeles, New York, and Toronto—with fifty-four young people, is a narrative of marginalized but resilient young people (Wolin and Wolin 1994), young people who were (and are) struggling to find the "right fit" while living in environments that were, more often than not, hostile to them because of Western society's bias against people who claim they are other than heterosexually oriented. It is only by immersing oneself in this fashion that one can begin to understand the discrepancies between the myths and misinformation about "gay and lesbian adolescents" and the realities of their experiences in the child welfare systems they live in. The narratives of ninety-six child welfare professionals, interviewed in all three cities, were also utilized to corroborate the stories of the young people.

Quotations are taken from the interviews described above. The names of all those interviewed are changed or omitted to insure confidentiality. The names of other individuals or the names of child welfare agencies mentioned in these narratives have also been changed to protect the confidentiality of the informants.

I have also written this book because I think that adolescents, particularly those who are members of oppressed groups, have a perspective that permits them—in fact, compels them—to consider the dominant norms of society from a distinct vantage point. These fifty-four young people are important informants not only about their own lives but also about the general socialization of gay and lesbian adolescents in U.S. and Canadian culture. Because they have experienced out-of-home care placements, they are able to offer insights into their individual care and the system as a whole. They are able to teach us about variations in the treatment of gay and lesbian adolescents since they come from a range of geographic locations. Their young lives offer a particularly rich source of information about their families, placement situations, and struggle toward adapting to a variety of environments by seeking to obtain a "good fit" across time.

Though gay/lesbian adolescents in child welfare settings are a topic about which different people have different opinions, these adolescents themselves have never been thoroughly studied. This book represents a first attempt to do so, to comprehensively examine and investigate the meaning and experiences of these young people. It is an early contribution to what I hope will be a wider inquiry that will expand over the next few decades.

Acknowledgments

In researching and writing *We Don't Exactly Get the Welcome Wagon* I have incurred debts of gratitude to many people. One of the most pleasant aspects in preparing the manuscript is the opportunity to thank them all within its pages.

A qualitative research design can only be as good as its informants. The people who assisted me most were the fifty-four brave young people I interviewed for this study. Their incredible inner strength, despite their difficult lives, not only moved me, but left me with a deep admiration for them. I wish to thank them for allowing me to tell their stories here.

My many colleagues in the child welfare field in New York City, in Toronto, particularly John McCullagh, Rob Travers, Marg Schneider, and Bev Liptzitz, as well as Terry de Crescenzo and her dedicated and loyal staff at GLASS in Los Angeles, also generously contributed to an understanding of the experience of gay/lesbian adolescents in child welfare settings.

There have been several people—good colleagues, good friends—who have also been closely connected with this book, and they deserve special mention:

John Michel, my editor at Columbia University Press makes writing for the Press a sincere pleasure.

Professor Irwin Epstein introduced me into grounded theory as a research process through which adequate sociological theory could be developed for application to social work problems and practices while I was a doctoral student at Hunter College School of Social Work. His intellectual influence, as well as his abundant generosity as a colleague, has been a significant part of this study from the beginning to the completion.

Sam Ross, Executive Director Emeritus of Green Chimneys Children's Services, with whom I have had the pleasure of being associated for the past ten years, has never wavered in his support and encouragement for me or for this project. When others worried about the implications of connecting gay and lesbian issues with child welfare issues, Sam never once said, "Gary, I think you went too far!" He always maintained confidence in me and gave his enthusiastic support. My thanks to him is inestimable, as my affection for him is immense.

My colleagues at the Columbia University School of Social Work in New York, several of whom read earlier drafts and provided thoughtful and generous feedback, have assisted me in completing this work by inviting me to a setting where the intellectual fervor and scholarly productivity are astounding. I have received indispensable encouragement and critique from Professors Alex Gitterman, Brenda McGowan, Barbara Simon, and Associate Dean Peg Hess. I am proud to be a part of the Columbia University School of Social Work community.

Finally, I have thought about where and how best on this list of acknowledgments to thank the people who lived with this book on a daily basis, but everything seems inadequate to describe how much they have helped. Mike Rendino, my partner, has provide me not only with a home environment that has been conducive to my own growth as a person, but also to good writing. His patience with me and my work is always laudable. I am also grateful for the love and the delight that Travis and Ian have brought to my life, I owe so much of my understanding for children and young people to them.

Correspondence may be sent to:
Professor Gerald P. Mallon
Columbia University School of Social Work
622 West 113th Street
New York N.Y. 10025
or via E-mail at gpm7@columbia.edu

We Don't Exactly Get the Welcome Wagon

| Introduction |

Members of historically denigrated groups have decades of direct experience in not being believed, in having their views of reality discounted by authorities whose own experiential truths are often discrepant wholly or in part from those of people who have grown up in the margins of society.

—Simon (1994:156)

Elbowed by the dominant culture into the margins of society, gay and lesbian adolescents, particularly those in out-of-home-care placements, have experienced firsthand the skepticism of those in positions of authority with respect to their experiences. Such doubt has caused these young people to develop an adeptness for growing up on the perimeter of mainstream society. The gay and lesbian young people interviewed for this study have experienced, firsthand, the skepticism of those in positions of authority about their very existence. Wilem, a 19-year-old from Los Angeles, expressed this viewpoint vigorously:

> If you live in a group home and you say that you're gay you are told that you are not gay and that you're going through a phase because you are a teenager. Or you're told that you are mixed up and that once you come out of this stage (you know as a teenager you are supposed to go through these stages), then you will not be gay. That's their attitude! If we know, that we know, that we know, that we know, that we know, that we know, that we are gay, they still tell us that we're not, it's just a phase. I think that they don't want to believe that young people can be gay.

Characterized by most professionals as a group of young people at risk, the narratives that follow suggest far more resilience than risk (Wolin and Wolin 1994).

We Don't Exactly Get the Welcome Wagon focuses on the multiple experiences of fifty-four gay/lesbian adolescents in U.S. and Canadian out-of-home child welfare systems. Initially, my aim was to write a straightforward description of these young peoples' lives in an out-of-home child welfare setting, and ideally, to try to see the world of gay/lesbian adolescents as they themselves see and experience that world. Later, when trying to make sense of my field notes and endless hours of transcribed interviews, I realized that another of my aims was to explain both to myself and others how these young people remained human in the face of often inhuman conditions. These marginalized youth frequently sensed that they were treated as less than human:

> I know that I did some things that were probably pretty fucked up in the group home, but I did not deserve to be treated the way I was. I would say that gay and lesbian kids in foster care are treated really, really fucked up, that's all I can think of, they are treated really bad, they are treated as "less than."

I came to see how inadequate it was to think of these individuals in one-dimensional, stereotypical terms such as youth who were "flamboyant" or "obvious," as incomplete persons deficient in morals and character, or even characterized as "young people with problems."

While some gay/lesbian adolescents might seem at first glance to fit into one or another such category, others clearly do not. Although many of the child welfare professionals whom I interviewed implied that they did not have gay or lesbian young people in their programs, in almost every interview with the young people themselves, I was struck by how highly visible they were to one another. The narratives of gays and lesbians in out-of-home care from all three cities (Los Angeles, New York, and Toronto) were strikingly similar except for some minor terminology differences such as "a crown ward" in Canada as compared to "a state ward" in New York and Los Angeles. Some may have indeed been very "flamboyant" or very "obvious" with respect to their gender-conforming or -nonconforming behaviors or attitudes, but they tended to be different in the same way, hence their likeness to one another. However, although their differences were apparent, each of them seemed to be dealing with similar issues in being gay or lesbian and being an adolescent living apart from their families in an out-of-home child welfare setting.

An important fact about them is that their apparent visibility notwithstanding, they are at best a minority population in a system already plagued by a myriad of practice, policy, and program issues (Besharov 1988; Fraser, Pecora, and Haapala 1991; Kamerman and Kahn 1990; Lindsey 1994; McGowan and Meezan 1983; Pecora, Whittaker, and Maluccio 1994; Pelton 1989; Rzepnicki and Stein 1985). For every young person I met in the four years I conducted this study, there were thousands of others who are invisible in child welfare agencies in the United States and Canada.

In the pages that follow, I have documented some of the hardships of being gay or lesbian in the child welfare system. When they could be found, I have also documented the positive experiences. I have tried to show that only through extraordinary efforts can an adolescent find a good fit as a gay or lesbian individual in a group home, and sometimes not even these efforts are enough.

The humanity of gay/lesbian adolescents is under constant threat because of the many myths and stereotypes that pervade their lives. Consequently, most of them are engaged in an unremitting struggle to maintain their personal dignity in the face of predominantly inhospitable environmental conditions. In the process of searching for a good fit within one's family, many have been disappointed when the fit they sought was not to be found there. Others looked to the child welfare system for help in survival. There, some have found the help they need. Others find it impossible to deal with the arbitrariness and irrationality of the child welfare system toward them and have even sought the "safety" of the streets as an alternative "living arrangement."

Although lesbian and gay adolescents essentially face all the conventional stressors of adolescence, they also encounter some which are unique to their status as marginalized individuals in society. As such, adaptations are necessary to achieve a "goodness of fit" between the person:environment (Germain and Gitterman 1980, 1996). It is this dilemma that serves as the theoretical framework for understanding lesbian and adolescents in a developmental context.

This book presents narratives of marginalized young people, struggling to find the "right fit" while living within environments that were more often than not hostile to them because they claimed to be other than heterosexual. Their experiences help us to begin to understand the discrepancies between the myths and misinformation about "gay and lesbian adolescents" and their realities in the out-of-home child welfare systems in which they live.

The Child Welfare System

Although this book specifically focuses on the experiences of gay and lesbian adolescents in out-of-home child welfare systems in the United States and Canada, the reality is that most gays/lesbians are not placed in out-of-home-care child welfare settings. In fact, the majority of them, like their nongay counterparts, remain at home with their families and never interface with the child welfare system.

Analogous to the experiences of their nongay counterparts, about one-third of the gays/lesbians interviewed for this study were placed in out-of-home care before the onset of their adolescence (Aldgate, Maluccio, and Reeves 1989:325). Of this group, the majority noted that they came into placement for many of the same reasons that other children are placed: family disintegration, divorce, death or illness of a parent, substance abuse, alcoholism, physical abuse, and neglect (Whittaker 1981). Less than one-third of the young people in this study reported that they came into care for reasons that were directly related to their sexual orientation. This fact contradicts the prevalent assumption that most gay and lesbian youth in care are thrown out of their homes when they come out or are found out.

Living apart from one's family is seldom easy. Forty-seven of the young people interviewed for this study lived in community-based group homes, one lived in a family-based foster home. Two had been recently discharged from group homes and were living independently, four identified their living situation as "on the streets."

Out-of-home child welfare systems have long been and continue to be an integral part of the child welfare continuum of services. The structures of these residential programs vary widely, from small community-based group homes and short-term respite care or shelter facilities to large congregate care institutions that provide long-term or custodial care. They all share one common feature in that they provide care for children and youth on a 24-hour-day basis (CWLA 1981; Whittaker 1985). Group Home programs, which is where the majority of young people in this study lived, are defined in terms which Whittaker (1981:618) identifies as lacking "precision in terms of their defining characteristics and functions." As a child welfare service, the Child Welfare League of America, which set standards of care to reflect best practices, defines group home services in the following manner:

The provision of care and treatment in an agency-owned or operated facility that assures the continuity of care and opportunity for community experiences, in combination with a planned group living program and specialized services, for small groups of children and youth whose parents cannot care for them adequately and who because of their age, problems, or stage of treatment, can benefit by such a program. Service elements include: 1) exploration to determine appropriate service, development of a plan for services, and preparation for placement; 2) work on behalf of or directly with children an youth during placement (including provision of facilities and the essentials of daily living, such as meals, clothing, arrangements for education, recreation, religion, medical-dental care; child care supervision, social work, psychiatry, psychology; special education, vocational, and employment counseling; 3) work with parents while child is in placement; 4) postplacement activities during readjustment period.

(CWLA 1981: xx-xxi)

The formal language of the Child Welfare and Adoption Assistance Act of 1980 (P.L. 96–272), the landmark legislation which sought to restructure the nation's out-of-home-care system by preventing the unnecessary placement of children and adolescents in care and by moving children toward permanence in a timely manner, maintained that a central goal of the child welfare system was to provide the "least restrictive environment" for each child or youth in need of services (Laird and Hartman 1985: xxiii). Adopting the science of ecology as a metaphor for child welfare practice, Laird and Hartman (1985) suggest that the intent of this legislation may be interpreted to mean the environment which is most free from bureaucratic and institutional features such as lack of intimacy and depersonalization, the environment closest to a natural caring and nutritive system for most children and youth—their biological family. As such, group homes provide a less restrictive level of care than do large institutional congregate care settings, but more structure than family-based foster homes.

Historically, group homes were staffed by a married couple in an effort to replicate a "family-like" environment. Although that model has generally fallen out of favor in many parts of the United States and Canada, in some localities this type of group home is still in use. Most group homes, however, are generally staffed by individual child care workers or counselors who are employed by an agency to work in shifts to cover the twenty-four hours in a day. Child care workers, the lowest paid and generally the least educated and trained of the child welfare practitioners, nonetheless play a very important role in the lives of young people in their charge.

The daily stress of working with adolescents and the poor pay make it especially difficult for staff to radiate empathy and compassion in their dealings with their charges. It also makes for a high turnover in staff. Social workers, who usually do not have offices in the group home location, do not generally have as intimate a relationship with the adolescents as they visit the home on a regular basis to provide counseling and to work with families. Group home programs are supervised by agency administrators who are supposed to insure that agency and legal guidelines are maintained. In most group home programs the director decides who shall be allowed in, who shall be discharged, and who shall stay and under what conditions. Most directors are also quick to point out that they are the sole and final judge of what is acceptable behavior in the group home.

Young people are generally clustered in group homes by gender and age. They are expected to attend school in the community, participate in household chores to maintain the environment of the facility, and adhere to a series of formal and informal rules that guide the program. In addition to observing the usual injunctions against alcohol, drugs, carrying weapons, fighting, and using abusive language, the residents of group homes are often required to sign contracts promising to modify their behavior by attending counseling sessions, attending independent living skills classes, getting up promptly in the morning, keeping their rooms clean, and simply "showing that you want to improve yourself." Most group homes for adolescents focus on preparing these young people for independent living on or before their twenty-first birthday in New York and Toronto and by their eighteenth in Los Angeles. Although most group homes are guided by rules and regulations promulgated by the state or province, each group home program has its own unique culture and norms. Some group homes are warm, loving, and accepting of diversity and some are unnurturing, cold, and rigid. The young gays and lesbians interviewed for this study lived in and spoke about both.

The Historic Response of Child Welfare Practitioners

Although often times their existence has been denied, the fact is that there have always been gay/lesbian young people in U.S. and Canadian out-of-home-care settings. It has often been difficult for professionals to discern their existence for two reasons: (1) many of them did not fit the gender nonconforming stereotypes that most practitioners thought signaled a gay or lesbian identity, and (2) gay and lesbian youth are socialized to "hide" their orientation (Martin 1982). Recognition of these marginalized young people is further impaired by the individual moral attitudes many child welfare professionals have that express contempt for homosexual orientation and by an almost complete lack of knowledge most professionals have about normal gay and lesbian adolescent development (Mallon 1997). Religious and cultural biases against gays and lesbians also play a large role in the disavowal of their existence.

Recent public debates about homosexuality both in the United States and Canada, however, have made it possible for child welfare professionals to begin to discuss these issues more candidly. In light of this greater openness, child welfare providers have increasingly become more aware that their clients included both gay and lesbian adolescents. Nonetheless, too many professionals still maintain that there are no gay or lesbian young people in their agencies, as reported by this staff member in New York:

> We don't have any residents who are gay or lesbian. We have over a hundred adolescents in our programs and I know all of them and none of them are gay or lesbian! We have never encountered any gay or lesbian adolescents in our programs and I have had calls inquiring about this population before and when I asked my social workers in the agency they said that they had never encountered any youngsters who were gay or lesbian. In some cases they had a few kids that they suspected might have been, but after they talked to them, they found out that they weren't.[1]

Although most of these adolescents are not in care *because* they are gay or lesbian, many of the child welfare professionals interviewed felt compelled to respond in some way to their sexuality, but were unsure of the appropriate way to do so. The majority of them revealed a great deal of ignorance about the experiences of gays/lesbians. Most wanted to know if these youngsters made a choice to be gay or lesbian. They wondered if they should encourage their gay/lesbian clients to "go straight" or if, in assisting them to obtain special services, professionals could be perceived as "encouraging" homosexuality or seen as "pushing them over the edge." With respect to residential or foster home placements, practitioners wondered about sleeping arrangements. Should they be placed with the same sex or opposite sex? Should they be placed by themselves or mainstreamed with other gay young people? Other staff wondered about what if these gay/lesbians made advances toward other residents, how would other residents react? Behind these questions lay a general feeling of uneasiness with homosexuality.

Myths and stereotypes about gays/lesbians are so pervasive in Western society that they are generally accepted as fact by most who are not gay or lesbian themselves or else do not know someone who is (Hunter and Schaechter 1987). Armed with very little accurate information about gay/ lesbian identity, most professionals rely on an abundance of myths, stereotypes, and misinformation as their only knowledge base. Because child welfare systems have not acknowledged the existence of these young people, policies to guide practice with them are also almost nonexistent, leaving practitioners to develop policies on their own.

The Young People in the Study

Fifty-four self-identified gays and lesbians, thirty-eight young men and sixteen young women, were interviewed by me between 1993 and 1995. They were between the ages of 17 and 21, were placed in out-of-home-care child welfare systems, and came from diverse ethnic, cultural, and social-class backgrounds. Twenty-seven lived in the New York City area; sixteen lived in the Los Angeles metropolitan area; eleven lived in Toronto. Like many children and youth placed in out-of-home care, their family histories were often painful and punishing.

From a distance, the young people appeared to be a fairly homogeneous group. They were from lower working-class and lower socioeconomic families. With few exceptions they were poor and did not have many marketable skills. But as one moved closer to them—close enough to see them as individuals—they appeared to be strikingly different from one another—more different, perhaps, than their nongay counterparts. Western society is more accepting of people who conform, people who are, in many ways, very much like one another—like students in a private high school or therapists trained by a particular psychotherapy institute.

There is a special stigma to being gay or lesbian in a world of presumed heterosexuality (labeled "heterocentrism" in this book). Heterocentrism is understood as a result of heterosexual privilege or heterocentrism and is analogous to racism, sexism, and other ideologies of oppression (Pharr

1988). Heterocentrism, which I feel most accurately describes the systemic display of gay and lesbian discrimination in a major social institutions—in this case the child welfare system—has as its primary assumption that the world is and should be heterosexual. This assumption, illustrated most clearly by heterosexual privilege, causes gay and lesbian individuals to engage in a constant search for a good fit between their individual nature, which is regarded as stigmatized by Western society (and usually by their families), and their environments, which are generally hostile and void of nutrients necessary for healthy growth.

Heterocentrism, paired with the taint of being placed in out-of-home care, in the words of Goffman (1963:5) "spoils the identity." Once one's identity is tainted, as described by those interviewed in this study, only three strategies are open to reduce the stigmatization.

One, the individual can attempt to correct the "deviant trait." (In the case of the gay or lesbian, he or she can attempt to "pass as heterosexual," i.e., dating opposite-gendered individuals or "talk up" actual or fictional histories of romance with opposite-gendered individuals.)

Two, the individual can invest energy in mastering activities considered in the normal course of things to be beyond what is expected of a "typical" adolescent. He/she can devote him/herself to excelling in academics, sports, or the arts—or engage in heterosexual promiscuity, e.g., young lesbians becoming pregnant or young gays fathering children.

Three, the individual can diverge from the mainstream and accept his/her identity by coming out and living as an openly gay or lesbian individual. These gays/lesbians proudly proclaim to themselves, and to the world, the dignity of their lives. The young people interviewed reported that at there were times that they had used all three of the strategies identified by Goffman, in some cases moving back and forth between them.

Many said they had tried to conform but failed. Others, particularly those who are gender-nonconforming in their behavior, dress, or mannerisms, are less able to conform to Western society's models for "compulsory heterosexuality" (Rich 1983). Their nonconformity took on many different shapes and most of them showed an remarkable flare for individuality. The composition of the final pool of fifty-four young people is outlined in table 1.1. For a complete discussion of the sampling procedure and process of selecting informants (young people and staff members), see appendix 1.

How does this group of fifty-four gays/lesbians in out-of-home care compare with an overall pool of U.S.-Canadian young people in out-of-

TABLE I Characteristics of Young People Interviewed, 1993–1995

CHARACTERISTIC	NUMBER	PERCENT
Race		
African American	22	41%
Latino/a	12	22%
Caucasian	15	28%
Indo-Caribbean	2	3.5%
Afro-Caribbean	2	3.5%
Aborigine Canadian	1	2%
Gender		
Male	38	70%
Female	16	30%
Age at interview		
17	16	30%
18	16	30%
19	10	18%
20	7	13%
21	5	9%
Education		
Completed high school	20	37%
Currently in high school	22	41%
Enrolled in college	3	5%
High school dropout	9	17%
Religion		
Protestant	31	57%
Catholic	21	39%
Two-Spirited	1	2%
Muslim	1	2%
Country of origin		
United States	43	80%
Canada	11	20%
Native-born	46	85%
Born in other countries[a]	8	15%
Residence most of life		
Rural	4	7%
Suburban	3	6%
Urban	47	87%
Living arrangement time of interview		
Group home	47	87%
Foster home	1	2%
Independent living	2	4%
Living on the streets	4	7%

[a] 2 each from Jamaica, Trinidad, Mexico; 1 each from Dominican Republic, Nicaragua.

home care? At the close of 1994 there were 468,000 adolescents in out-of-home care in the United States (U.S. House 1996: 743–44). Of this total, New York and California, the states with the most children placed, had 60,216 and 87,368 respectively. Canada's out-of-home-care population in 1995 was significantly lower—7,569. Ontario, the largest Canadian province and the province where this study was conducted, had the greatest number of young people in care—2,807: 17- and 18-year-olds in out-of-home care, from all parts of Canada, comprised 739 of the total group (Statistics Canada 1995: 5). In 1995, the Children's Aid Society in Toronto provided out-of-home-care services for 2,534 children; of that population, 431 were adolescents living in community or semi-independent programs (CASMT 1995a).

Racially the group has a larger proportion of black, Latino, aboriginal, and Caribbean residents (72%, n=28) than overall U.S. or Canadian percentages of youths in out-of-home-care placements (Child Welfare League of America 1995). I purposefully included larger populations of people of color for two reasons: to reflect the higher proportions of children of color in the child welfare systems and to insure the inclusion of perspectives too rarely solicited and too often presumed to be identical and similar to those of Caucasian heterosexual adolescents.

Educationally, 22% of the sample was in high school; 20% had completed high school; 5% were in college, 17% had dropped out of school. The rate of noncompletion of high school for youths in this study (17%) was more favorable than the noncompletion rate of 24.5% reported by the U.S. Department of Education (Children's Defense Fund 1995) for a comparable group of young people in the United States and Canada.

The religious identification of these young people was similar in most respects to both countries' pool of young people in this age range. The overwhelming majority, 98% (n=53), identified as Christian, one person identified as two-spirited, another as Muslim. Jews and young people from other faiths are not represented in this sample and similarly are underrepresented in the out-of-home-care systems of Canada and the United States (U.S. House 1996; Statistics Canada 1997).

The percentage of foreign-born in the group, 15%, was larger than the general population of young people ages 14 and above. The preponderance of urban dwellers, 87% (n=47), was reflective of the proximity to large cities where young people were interviewed.

With respect to sexual orientation, all of those interviewed were self-identified as gay or lesbian. Males indicated that they first became aware of their gay sexual orientation at a mean age of 10 years, four youngsters indicated that they always knew. Girls reported that they developed a sense of awareness at a later age, the mean age being 13 years.

The age distribution of this group favors the younger end of the range. Gays/lesbians in the range of 20 to 21 years are underrepresented here, which is reflective of the fact that child welfare services terminate at age 18 in California and Ontario. California's out-of-home-care population between the ages of 12 and 19 represents only 26.7% of the total foster care population. New York State's adolescent population is a comparable figure—29.1% of the total out-of-home-care population (U.S. House 1996: 743–44). The majority of the young people discussed here, 78 percent (n=42), were between the ages of 17 and 19.

Although the young people in the upper age groups were not in care at the time of the interview, the fact that 50% (n=27) of the sample indicated that they had at one point in their placement lived on the streets as an alternative to living in a group home, coupled with the fact that both groups had spent a considerable amount of time in out-of-home care, their experiences added immeasurably to the value of the study. The average length of stay for males was nine years. The average length of stay for females was three years. The large majority of the pool of young people, 89% (n=48), reported that they had multiple placements. The overall mean number of placements was 5.3. The mean number of years in placement was almost equal to that number (5.4 years). The number of multiple placements ranged from 2 to 38 different out-of-home arrangements. The figures from this study, in all three areas, are comparable to figures I gathered from prior research (Mallon, in press) with a comparable sample size and adolescent population of young people in out-of-home care and others (Cook 1988; Maluccio and Fein 1985; Meston 1988).

Some Notable Young People

Brief biographies of the fifty-four young people, abstracted from their (taped and transcribed) life histories, are presented in appendix 2. In the interviews, the language with which these young people [who are the focus of the study, in the interviews] expressed their beliefs and described their lives ranged from modern-day standard English to urban street-argot and their own unique gay/lesbian slang that speaks to the distinctive experiences of growing up in the margins. For the fifteen or so young people who appear most frequently in this book, short sketches from their life histories, given in appendix 2, are presented here to introduce them, alphabetically, to the reader. Here and throughout the book, the years 1993 and 1995, when most of the life histories were taken, are all to be considered the historical present.

Angelo is a 17-year-old Mexican American who identifies as gay. He speaks in heavily accented English, with a strong Mexican inflection in his voice. He is stocky in stature with dark features. Angelo has been in several Los Angeles agencies but was finally placed, at his lawyer's request, in a gay-affirming group home. Angelo reports that he was unmercifully teased by peers in his other group homes after gay-oriented magazines were discovered in his room. He has been in placement since he was 12 years old. Angelo sometimes dresses in opposite-gendered clothing, called cross-dressing. About this he says, "I didn't have the freedom to cross dress in the other places. Here being gay, cross-dressing is not an issue, this place helps individuals to know who they are. Whatever the issue here, people are accepting." About his experience in the group home he says, "Places like this help people to accept others as they are. It helps you build self-esteem. It's a home away from home." His mother is deceased and his father was unable to care for him and his three siblings, who are now cared for by an aunt who cannot accept Angelo's gay identity.

Gerald, 20 years old, was born in Trinidad. He dresses in punk style with a dramatic spiked and multicolored hairstyle. He wears spiked bracelets and other punk-identified jewelry. He is a formidable and threatening-looking young man who has, at his own admission, adopted such a style of fashion to deter others from, as he put it, "messin' with me." Gerald has been in several congregate care placements, leaving the last one to live on the streets when a friend, who also lived there, was killed by another resident because she refused to give him a cigarette. Gerald said: "If she got killed for doing that, imagine what they would do to me if they found out that I was gay." After four months of living on the streets, he was referred by his social worker to a gay-affirming residence where he currently resides.

Jason is a well-built, attractive 18-year-old African American. He plays football for his high school. He said "Most people would never believe that I am gay, because I am not their stereotype of what being gay is . . .but I am." Jason came into placement when he was 14 because he was arrested for getting into a fight with another teenager. Since Jason is a gender-conforming adolescent male, he rarely has had any difficulty with staff or peers about his sexuality, but he is not open with anyone on the staff about his gay identity. Jason reports: "I have gay friends and we hang out, but that's outside the group home. I keep my business to myself because if you are open in the group home, they tear you up. I've seen it happen before. I'd rather stay hidden."

Katrina is a 21-year-old Aborigine Canadian who identifies as lesbian. Katrina is proud of her "first person" status. She has been placed in several out-of-home placements since the age of six months. She describes her experience as "a mixture of things, being in a group home and then leaving and hanging out on the streets and going back and staying there for a bit, so it was like a back and forth kind of thing. When the decision was made to move me then I would go to the next place but I was always running away, going back and then running away again. . . . It was hard in some ways because if I said I was a lesbian, it was always denied. If I said 'I'm a lesbian,' they said, 'oh, no you're not,' it was hard. Actually, they either denied it or never said anything." Katrina is of medium build, with dark straight hair. She is extraordinarily quick-witted and a great storyteller.

Kevin is a 20-year-old Caucasian. He is small in stature, of Irish ancestry, and very hyperactive, as evidenced by the fact that he could not sit still throughout the interview. Kevin recalls that his mother was unable to care for him and his siblings and consequently they were placed in a series of foster homes. Kevin estimates that he was in about nine different foster homes. "Some were good, some were bad." He says, however, that he would never go back to them—he is now living on his own. "They treated gay kids there really bad. They didn't know about me, because I'm not very effeminate, but I saw what they did to the other gay kids who couldn't hide."

Maria is a Latina. She was born in Mexico and is 20 years old. She is about 5'2" with long brown hair and copper-colored skin. She entered care when she was 10 and lived in a series of foster homes, pre-adoptive homes, and ultimately in several group homes. She came "into the life" as she puts it, when she was 17. Maria has a wonderful philosophy of life: "People need to be themselves, just forget what other people say—people are always gonna have something to say whether you're gay or straight, but if you be yourself—you'll be okay." She currently lives on her own. Her parents are deceased.

Maura is an 18-year-old Caucasian who, when asked how she identified, said: "I prefer to be called a dyke." Maura was psychiatrically hospitalized after a bout with depression and a suicide attempt that she now attributes to an increasing isolation due to her emerging lesbian identity. After several unsuccessful placements in inhospitable environments which resulted in her running away from the facilities, Maura is currently placed in a group home in New York City where she feels accepted, though not wholly understood, by most staff and peers. Maura is very verbal, short in stature, and sports an equally short haircut.

Paula is a 20-year-old Caucasian Canadian. She has been in multiple placements and has lived in group homes, foster homes, and shelters. Paula came into placement because she had problems getting along with her mother. Reflecting on her experiences in group homes she said: "Sometimes things that go on in group homes are not that blatant, but some things are really blatant, sometimes people just refuse to talk to you. People in the system don't know how to deal with it. . . . when counselors get turned out of universities they run into things that they don't know how to deal with. And it just so happens that working with gay kids is one of those things. But nobody teaches you . . . there's some information out there but it's not like a university course. They don't know how to counsel Gay Students 101."

Peter, aged 18, and his brother **John**, aged 17, are African Americans. Both brothers are tall and wiry, with short hair. After their mother abandoned them, they were begrudgingly taken in to live with their aunt, who is described by the brothers as being "very religious." Their aunt threw them out of her home when she "found out" that they were gay after reading letters that they had received from same-gendered friends. Peter and John lived on the streets in Los Angeles for several months before entering the child welfare system. John recalls knowing he was gay this humorous way: "I knew that I was gay when I saw Bruce Willis and I thought, oh, my! That's when I knew."

Richard is a 17-year-old African American. He is tall and overweight. He has a joking manner and flirts outrageously throughout the interview. He was in several placements before coming to the group home. "I got to come here because I'm gay." He said, "I got interviewed and they accepted me—people in other places weren't comfortable with differences. My social worker was a lesbian and she referred me here." Philip's family had a hard time accepting him: "My mother's boyfriend was abusive towards me. My grandmother couldn't deal with me either. You know those church people have a really hard time with gay people, even their own family. Oh Jesus, oh, glory—the regular old religious family. They make me crazy. If they are so into God and God is love and all then we should treat each other better. They say that God don't make no mistake. It was no mistake to make me a gay black man."

Sharice is a 19-year-old African American. She is attractive and dresses with a flair. There is an instant recognition of self-confidence about her and she commands instant respect from everyone she encounters. After being in "too many group homes to remember" and after a staff member in one, according to Sharice, raped her, she left care and refused to return.

Tamil is an 18-year-old African American who has been in a group home placement in New York City for three years. He was placed because his grandmother, with whom he lived, could not "deal with" his gay life. This is his first placement. He is tall, of slender build, and is a very flashy dresser who frequently experiments with innovative hair designs. His appearance, together with his assertive character, suggests to newcomers that he is very confident about himself. He is, as he notes, "quick to throw shade" (to verbally defend oneself) and extremely outspoken about the rights of gay youths. He is, according to his reports and other youths interviewed for this study, frequently seen by other young people as their spokesperson.

Tina is a 20-year-old, born in Trinidad. She has been in several group home placements in Toronto. She is extremely articulate and able to point out both the positive and negative elements of her experience as a young person in an out-of-home child welfare placement. She also reflects about the need to hide: "I think there's lots of gay and lesbian kids in care, but they hide, they hide for the same reasons I did. They may not be out but they are there. When we do come out, it's difficult, because when we do we are treated like we have a psychiatric problem. It is the discrimination that we face that effects us, most just being gay, lesbian, bisexual." Although she did not come out in her group home, she came out as soon as she left care. Tina reflects on the negative associations that her culture had toward gay and lesbian persons: "I have no family network for support. I am Trinidadian and it was very very taboo, very anti-lesbian or gay. There was no connection and no networking from my family. We can't go to our community that way." Tina is currently living on her own, attending college, and employed full time.

Tracey is an 18-year-old light-skinned African-American. He was placed by his aunt after he developed behavior problems in school, which he now identifies as reaction to his emerging gay identity. Tracey has been in three group homes, has lived on the streets, in subway tunnels, and in one congregate care facility in upstate New York. Tracey's story is filled with verbal and physical abuse and sadness. His quote, "We don't exactly get the Welcome Wagon when we come to a group home," provides the title for this book.

Wilem is a 19-year-old Latino. This is his first placement; he has never lived on the streets and feels lucky that he has been placed in this affirming group home in Los Angeles. He was placed because "My parents couldn't deal with my sexuality. They'd say: 'ok you are . . . . but let's not talk about it, let's leave it where it is.' They just went into shock, saying it was a phase, 'what did we do wrong'—the usual thing. I tried to talk about it with them but they didn't want to talk about it and if they couldn't deal with that then they couldn't deal with me and I left my home." After leaving home he claimed "I moved in with a friend and my parents harassed me to come back and I tried to kill myself because I didn't want to deal with it. My social worker refer me to the Gomphers Residence which has been okay for me"

What follows is a portrait of fifty-four nonconformists. As gays and lesbians they were invisible to most or, more impertinently, treated as if they didn't exist, the young people in this study insisted on living openly, boldly, and in most cases proudly as gays or lesbians. They violated the tacit agreement that society has perpetrated—homosexuality is something that we should not talk about; and consequently, as we shall see in the chapters ahead, they have endured both the social stigma that gay and lesbian people face, but also, in some cases, were successful in finding the right fit. They pushed against the closet door, some with great force and some with barely enough strength to crack it open. Most have done so with an intensity and regard that smash the conventional myths and stereotypes that have fallaciously characterized gay and lesbian people. As they have reported, to be a gay or lesbian or to be perceived to be one, is to be characterized as someone who has stepped out of line.

CHAPTER 1

| The Road to Acceptance |

Theoreticians who espouse the normative position of adolescence (Offer, Ostrov, and Howard 1981; Offer and Offer 1975) propose that youth is a time of physical and cognitive development, psychological growth, and the development of life plans. This perspective, which avoids focusing on the crisis mode of the developmental processes of the period, holds that most adolescents cope successfully with the adaptive tasks of puberty and adolescence (Germain 1991:354).

Since heterocentric assumptions dominate the environments of lesbian and gay adolescents, there is no acceptable way to achieve adulthood as either defined by traditional theories (Blos 1981; Erikson 1950; Marcia 1980; Newman and Newman 1987) or by social and environmental expectations. Most theories of adolescent development assume heterosexuality. Maria, one of the young woman interviewed for this study, spoke directly to these assumptions when she said:

> You're constantly raised to think heterosexism is right and gay is wrong— so you think it's wrong. The other kids in the group home follow the crowd and then behind closed doors they want to check it out with you.

Indeed, Western culture's negative myths, stereotypes, and misconceptions about gays and lesbians (rather than the orientation itself) create the major life stressor for young lesbian, gay, or bisexual people. Being attracted to someone of the same sex embodies a sense of fit that is not only expressed through same-sex sexual behavior, but also, through a sense of internal goodness of fit, expressed emotionally and affectionally. In fact, homosexuality can be defined using the same terms employed to define heterosexuality—"the emotional and physical attraction to persons of opposite sex; including falling in love, caring for, and making a commitment to another person" (Schneider 1988:18). Unfortunately, the public focuses exclusively on the sexual aspects of homosexuality and homosexually oriented people become labeled solely for their sexuality. The very descriptor "homosexual" obscures everything else about a person (Schneider 1988). Homosexuality differs from heterosexuality only in that the object of attraction is a person of the same sex.

Unlike their heterosexual counterparts, young gays and lesbians must learn to juggle two interrelated processes at the same time—growing up and coming out (Hetrick and Martin 1987; Hunter and Schaecher 1987; Schneider 1988). Coming out, a distinctively homosexual phenomenon, is defined as a developmental process through which gay and lesbian people recognize their sexual orientation and integrate this knowledge into their personal and social lives (De Monteflores and Schultz 1979:59). Several researchers and practitioners (Cass 1979, 1984; Coleman 1981; Minton and McDonald 1984; Troiden 1979, 1993) have conceptualized coming out within a developmental framework that unfolds in stages. One four-stage model, incorporating and elaborating on other previous models, is proposed by Troiden (1993).

Troiden (1988) proposes a four-stage coming out model. In the first stage, Sensitization, one has a general feeling of being marginal and different from others. In the second stage, Identity Confusion, one begins to entertain the thought that he/she might be gay/lesbian. In the third stage, Identity Assumption, one begins to identify with being gay or lesbian. The final stage, Commitment, culminates in the development of positive feelings about being gay or lesbian as one begins to integrate this identity into other social and personal arenas. Although stage models are useful in theoretically understanding a process, in fact, this process, like most other life processes, infrequently progresses in an orderly or invariable manner.

The events which mark coming out and the pace of this process vary from person to person. Consequently, some young people move through the process smoothly, accepting their sexuality, making social contacts, and finding a good fit within their environments. Others are unnerved by their sexuality, vacillating in their conviction, hiding in their uneasiness, and struggling to find the right fit.

Three general patterns of coming out emerged from the variety of these fifty-four individuals' experiences. Some expressed that they have always had a sense of being gay or lesbian. Others appear to switch rather abruptly from a heterosexual to a homosexual orientation, usually as a result of meeting someone who helps them to see that they are not sick or deviant. Still others vacillate between a heterosexual and a gay or lesbian orientation until arriving at a determination.

Knowledge about the coming out process is important in developing an understanding of gay and lesbian adolescents because as self-acceptance increases, so does the internal "goodness of fit" process that enhances one's capacity to self-disclose to others (Olsen and King 1995). Notwithstanding research that suggests gay and lesbian young people are disclosing at earlier ages (Herdt and Boxer 1993), not all gay or lesbian individuals come out as adolescents. Some may come out later in life, while others may choose to spend a lifetime hiding or repressing their orientation.

For a lesbian or gay youth, the realization that one is attracted to someone of the same sex can be a very confusing time. Confusion, although uncomfortable, is a normal part of adolescent development (Schneider and Tremble 1987). As different environments and normal life stresses may require new energies or new adaptations, many adolescents do not resolve the issue of sexual orientation until their early twenties when they are in college or in the world of work. Lesbians and gays do not choose their sexual feelings. They do choose how they will act on them (Cain 1991).

Although gays and lesbians share many common characteristics, there are distinct differences between the two (De Monteflores and Schultz 1978; Schneider 1989). The differences are more likely attributed to gender than to sexual orientation. For example, the young men interviewed reported that they came out at age 10 while women reported the development of self-awareness three years later, at age 13. This suggests that there are differences in the process that are bound by gender and perhaps by social conventions. Hunter and Schaecher (1987) also note that gay males tend to come out earlier, and indicate that they seem to focus on the physical aspects of sexuality. Young lesbians, on the other hand, are more likely to come out later and to form intense relationships with each other (Gramick 1984; Peplau 1991; Ponse 1988; Reiter 1991; Smart 1989; Sophie 1985/1986). Gays or lesbians of color, who represent the majority in this study (72%), report having had an even more difficult time managing their sexual identity as they have already had to deal with the onerous effects of racial or ethnic discrimination. In self-identifying as gay or lesbian, they must also choose to openly address or ignore a supplementary status that is generally regarded as marginal (Savin-Williams and

Rodriguez 1993; Tremble, Schneider, and Appathurai 1989). Tina, a Trinidadian from Canada, spoke openly about this experience:

> It's definitely really, really, difficult, as a lesbian woman of color. I have multiples of these difficulties—the same racism that is there in general society, is in gay communities. It multiplies the oppression I feel. It doubles it—if it's not one, it's the other. The only way we become visible is to accept ourselves openly and then become visible, but as a woman of color there are even more issues to contend with.

Although much has beeen written about the vulnerability of gay/lesbian adolescents (Gonsiorek 1988; Hetrick and Martin 1987; Hunter and Schaecher 1987, 1990, 1994; Remafedi 1987a, 1987b), many of these young people show a remarkable resilience (Savin-Williams 1995). Learning to negotiate a dual identity in a hostile environment is undoubtedly stressful, yet those who successfully move through the hostility emerge as resourceful and empowered individuals.

Sensing Being Different

I knew that I was different, no one ever told me, but I just knew.

For many of the young people interviewed for this study, the journey into adolescence began with the development of a sense of being "different." In various ways, young people articulated the importance of recognition of their identity. Steven, a 17-year-old from New York, viewed this process as beginning with the development of a sense of differentness when quite young:

> I remember feeling different at a young age, about four or five actually. I don't mean that I knew I was different sexually, I just knew I was different. But I saw how my family acted, they let me know that my difference was not acceptable.

Although U.S.-Canadian society would generally prefer to think of children as innocent, nonsexual entities, children are indeed sexual beings (Constantine and Martinson 1981; Jackson 1982). Whitlock (1989:20) notes: "It is easy to lose sight of the fact that sexuality is a component of human personality that is already developing in a child's earliest years."

Retrospective studies, in fact, found that some lesbian and gay adults recalled experiencing a sense of "differentness" as early as age four (Bell et al. 1981; Cantwell 1996; Coleman 1986; Hunter and Schaecher 1987; Mallon 1994a).

Similarly, Patrick, a 17-year-old from California, held out this vivid recollection as a key element of his identity:

> I knew I was different at age four. I remember being attracted to my preschool teacher. I saw him and thought "he's cute" and I just remember looking at his legs and thinking to myself—"what a man!"

Children at ages four or five begin to be socialized to recognize gender role behavior (Constantine and Martinson 1981; Diamond 1981; Diepold and Young 1979; Newman and Newman 1987) and to develop interests in what "Moms do" and what "Dads do." A child who will later identify as lesbian or gay might also begin to sense an attraction to same sex individuals during this period. In fact, many gay and lesbian adults have felt since childhood that there was something different about them, something they couldn't name and didn't understand, but knew that they must intuitively not reveal. Kevin, a Caucasian 20-year-old from New York, recollected:

> I knew that I was different from the others in my family and from other boys, but I didn't know what it was that I felt. Some part of me though knew that I should not tell anyone about this feeling because people in my family were very clear about what boys did and what girls did. I always wanted to do what the girls did, but that behavior was frowned upon, so I just kept those feelings to myself.

At first, most children do not understand this difference, but they sense that they are not like others in their family.

For some children, though not all, as gender atypical behavior does not necessarily indicate one's sexual orientation, this sense of differentness is manifested by gender-nonconforming behaviors or by expressing gender-nonconforming ideas. Alex, an 18-year-old from Toronto, put it this way:

> I was about seven years old when I first felt different. I remember having crushes on boys and in second grade, it went away and I started to like girls. I knew that I was different, no one ever told me, but I just knew. To be honest, I didn't know what I was, but I felt different.

Kevin concurred:

> I knew I was different from other kids when I was five years old. I remember my sister got a Barbie for Christmas and I really wanted one too. When I told my family that I wanted a Barbie, my uncle got furious with me and said, "Boys, do not play with dolls, girls do!" I didn't care what he said, I still wanted a Barbie and for my birthday, my grandmother bought me a Ken doll (Barbie's boyfriend). I was disappointed, I still wanted Barbie, but I felt better knowing that at least she tried. This time my uncle was even more enraged. He said, "You are as queer as a three-dollar bill." I remember thinking I didn't even know they made three dollar bills, and I had no idea why he was so angry. But I quickly learned that whatever this was that I was feeling, I should keep it to myself because it just made people too upset.

When young people acted on or verbalized their feelings, they usually found that their behaviors or gender-nonconforming expressions were quickly squelched by a distressed relative or family member. James, an 18-year-old African American from New York City recalled how his mother made an issue of his perceived difference:

> My mother would say things like: "Can't you just be like the other boys? Can't you stop walking like that, talking like that"—or whatever it was that I was bothering her by doing. It was always this kind of thing. At that point, I didn't understand what she was saying, when she said I was acting "like that," I didn't see myself doing anything that was different from what any of the other little boys were doing. But she saw a difference and she would always criticize the way I did things. A lot of things that I just naturally did irked her. I thought I was just acting normal.

Others also remarked that they intuitively sensed they should not verbalize these feelings within their family systems.

> I always admired my sister's dolls, but I knew that I could never ask for one because my father would have gone crazy. So used to secretly go in my room and make paper dolls from plain white paper. I would cut them out and make paper hair for them, then I'd play with them. Since they were made from paper, I could crumple them up quickly and throw them away if anyone came into my room and asked me what I was doing. I'm not sure why I played with them, but somehow, I associated them with my feeling different and I really enjoyed them.

Negative familial responses or fear of them sends strong, clear messages of disapproval to a young person. These messages convey that this type of "difference" is not acceptable, as Wilem, a 19-year-old from Los Angeles noted:

> Be like all of the other kids, do not deviate too far from what your gender expects you to do. Don't attract attention to yourself or your family by being perceived as being different.

To discover innate difference when peer acceptance is paramount can be very overwhelming and confusing. But the cause of the fear is not only derived from the realization of difference; the fears also arise from the recognition that you might be one of "them," as this quote from Michelle suggests:

> My mother was always talking about "those people," she made lesbian sound as if they were the worst kind of people on earth. Imagine how I felt when I realized that the reason that I felt different was because I was "one of them."

Responding to this "difference," those interviewed reported receiving implied or conspicuous messages from their families and from society that this "difference" was not appropriate or not condoned. In most cases, they succumbed to familial and societal pressures and suppressed their difference. It resurfaces for many, however, during adolescence, as Peter's remark suggests:

> I'd say I was probably ten or twelve when I first knew, but I never had any experiences until I was about thirteen, but I have known for a while, I knew I was different.

Adaptations to Identity

> I started to work at hiding my difference. I was real good at hiding. I wanted to make sure that no one knew my secret.

Most young people internalize Western society's ideology of sex and gender at an early age and also have firsthand opportunities to observe society's dislike and disapproval of lesbians and gays. A child of four or five, feeling different from other members of the family, in many cases tacitly or implicitly told not to be different, determines via negative transactions within the milieu, that there is not a goodness of fit with the environment. As all children are eager to please their parental figures, most develop adaptations that assist them in masking their difference. This process, labeled as "passing" by some (Berger 1990; Brown 1991; Goffman 1963), is more appropriately described as "hiding" for children and adolescents (Martin 1982; Mallon 1994a).

Living within an environment that is hostile to their existence promotes stress, and this causes many lesbian/gay youths to search for ways to integrate their identities. These adolescents are faced with four choices as they begin to realize that they are part of a stigmatized and despised population (Martin 1982; Mallon 1994). They can hide, they can attempt to change their orientation, they can claim to be split on the middle ground of bisexuality, or they can accept their gay or lesbian identity.

Hiding: The young person who hides and represses same-sex sexual desires chooses the most elementary and least satisfactory adaptation to an emerging homosexual orientation. While the repressed youngster may successfully "push down" his or her gay or lesbian feelings during adolescence, these impulses for some may resurface later in life (see Malyon 1982). The adaptation of hiding leads to dysfunctional and distorted relationships. Lesbian and gay adolescents reported feeling inauthentic, "as if we are living a lie," feeling that others "would not accept us if they knew the truth." The pressure to conform creates a false sense of self (Shernoff and Finnegan 1991). Maura, an 18-year-old from New York, recalls this feeling of trying to fit in:

> I always had to make sure that I was not acting too butch or dressing too much like a dyke. I always felt like I was trying to be someone who I wasn't, always trying to fit in where I knew I didn't fit. A lot of people try to deny that they are gay. I just don't understand why it is that people can't accept it. It's hard though, they are afraid if they tell someone that they are in the life that they are gonna lose their friendship. In a group home it's hard to tell someone, it's even hard to tell a friend, you don't want to lose a friend.

Hiding is a destructive falsehood for lesbians and gays. Martin (1982:58) notes: "The socialization of the gay adolescent becomes a process of deception at all levels. This strategy of deception distorts almost all relationships the adolescent may attempt to develop or maintain and creates a sense of isolation." Alejandro, a 17-year-old from New York, illustrates Martin's poignant observation in this quote:

> I had friends, but none of them ever really knew me. I had a family, but they didn't know me either. I was always keeping a part of me—secret. God forbid anyone ever called me a faggot—I was devastated. I was so hurt, because deep inside I knew that it was true and I was terrified that maybe someone could tell. I hated my life. I felt like such a big fake.

Hiding and a false identity necessitates hyper-vigilance, i.e., the constant scanning of the environment for negative signals. Gays and lesbians become experts at self-monitoring their conscious and automatic behaviors. Kevin's comments point to the chronic stress associated with having to watch how you talk, stand, carry your books, use your hands, or how you dress—until it becomes unbearable:

> I always carried my books like the girls did. I don't know why, it just felt right. But in junior high I started to get really harassed about it and then I conformed. I carried my books like the guys. It wasn't that it felt right, I just had to—if I didn't they made my life miserable.

As adolescents shift from family-centered to peer-focused socialization, many begin to feel a normal distancing from their families. However, gay/lesbian adolescents may experience an abnormal distancing for fear that their parents will discover their secret. Janet, an 18-year-old Latina, recalled:

> I always got along pretty good with my mother but when I started to explore who I was, she started to ask too many questions and I kind of closed down. I felt bad, but I didn't feel ready to tell her I was a lesbian and I wasn't sure that she would be able to deal with it.

Hiding from family members and peers and living a falsehood, the lesbian or gay adolescent pays a "great psychological price, a very high anxiety, in living a life that can collapse at any moment" (Goffman 1963:87). Internalizing homophobia (Finnegan and McNally 1987; Malyon 1981; Pharr 1988) generates depression and anxiety. Albert, a 20-year-old from Toronto, recounted this clear experience:

> My mother died when I was thirteen and my father remarried six months after. And the family just couldn't deal with it. I couldn't deal with it. And

I tried suicide and a lot of other destructive things. I mean growing up was hard, my hormones were changing and although I never tried it I often thought of gay sex. But because I was brought up strict Roman Catholic it was tough. I was very scared because you know I was from a red-neck town and being gay was like, I couldn't handle it. Because of the loss of my mother, I don't know a lot of stress, I got very, very depressed. As I got older through high school, it started to get even worse because I'd attempted suicide many times. It was too much. It was like at first I did it because I wanted people to say hey look, you know, look at me, pay attention to me. But after that I was placed at St. Jude's, and that's when I started to realize and accept that I was gay.

Laurence told a similar story:

Society doesn't accept it, they are really against it. You don't know who you can talk to and you keep things bottled up inside and sometimes I thought I was going crazy. You think something is wrong with you. I mean it seems like every time they find out about me that it's a big deal and they can't deal with it. I just don't know, sometimes. It's so hard to be gay. I try to hide it, but sometimes I can't.

Hiding consumes a great deal of energy and produces undue stress, particularly if you are living in a group home, as Trevor remembered:

As a teenager in the system, you have to get a lot of things set up. Having to hide the fact that you are gay adds to the pressure. But because the pressure is not here at The Meadows you are able to function considerably better than if you had to keep it under wraps. You are able to put the effort which you would put into hiding, into more constructive things.

Changing: Some young people spoke about "changing," but their idea of change was in response to pressure from societal stigmatization, not because they were uncomfortable with their orientation. Joyce, a 21-year-old lesbian currently living independently made this astute observation:

I have heard some people say that people choose to be gay. To be honest, if I had a choice I would not have chosen to be gay. Who in the world would choose to go through all of the name-calling, all of the bashings, and all of the other crap that gay people have to go through every day?

Those who suppress gay or lesbian identity during adolescence declare a temporary developmental deferral. They often exhibit identity formation that is cropped as they attempt to "fit into" the heterosexual culture by adopting its values and role expectations. As Sharice explained:

> Staff didn't know I was gay because at the time I tried to keep it to myself because I didn't know how people would react toward me being gay, so that was like a dark side of me, I would just keep it to myself, I wouldn't let nobody know, I would pretend I liked guys and I would go out with them, but deep in my heart, I knew I wanted to be with a female.

Tina spoke about her internal sense of fit with respect to dating:

> At twelve or thirteen, I didn't know. I knew basically that I was a lesbian when I got to high school, when people were talking about dating and I thought it was silly and it didn't work for me. When I dated boys, it didn't feel right for me. Then I met a woman and we started dating and then I thought—"Oh, that's what everyone's talking about"—then it felt right.

Maura's comments speak to the same issue with great conviction:

> I first became aware of my feeling for women at a very young age. My attraction toward women was very gradual—having little crushes on girls—eventually it grew stronger and eventually I wanted it to be sexual—it became so overwhelming that it became a part of my life that I can no longer ignore or refuse to deny.

James reportedly refrained from dating altogether:

> I was really into school. No one knew who I was because I kept it hidden. I only had time for school—I didn't date, I didn't hang out, I just read and studied. In the long run it was all right, but I guess looking back it should have been a time when I was dating and seeing people, rather than studying all the time.

Frequently this adaptive choice is expressed through overachievement, overcompensating for feelings of inadequacy and unacceptableness. Some young people may attempt to brace the suppression of gay or lesbian feelings by involvement in heterosexual marriage; others make superhuman efforts to become the "perfect" child or the "best little girl or boy in the world" (Reid 1973). Treg, an 18-year-old African-American from New York, was a perfect example of this type of young person:

> I made sure that I was excellent in school, excellent at home, I never made trouble. I made sure that I was so excellent that so it could camouflage the real me.

Sexual feelings are sublimated into positive or negative obsessions— sports, academics, clubs, computers, or drugs, alcohol, and involvement in other high-risk behaviors. Raul noted how changing creates a state of chronic unrest and disequilibrium:

> I started to smoke a lot of weed and to get high a lot. You name it I did it, pot, acid, ecstasy, speed . . . I did it all. I just wanted to kill the loneliness I felt inside. I really didn't care if I lived or died. Trying to deal with my identity was a really difficult time for me and I guess I didn't always deal with it very well.

Each of these changes, however, point to negotiating life within a hostile environment, where young people cannot be themselves and where they are constantly searching for a good fit. The comments of Mike, a 19-year-old Latino from New York, held out the hope that a good fit was possible:

> I was literally making myself sick. I wasn't eating, I didn't talk to my family, I cut school, I got high. I was a mess when I was first coming to terms with who I was. I was very depressed and I often wondered if it was even worth living, but one day I met this guy at school. He was open about who he was, he didn't care. I, of course, was interested in getting to know him, because he was like I thought I was, but I was scared too. One day we talked, and then we got to be friends. He told me I wasn't crazy, I wasn't sick, I wasn't evil—he said I was fine just the way I was. He literally saved my life.

Hiding and changing, as these narratives explicate, are common to the process of coming to terms with a gay or lesbian identity. To hide a basic component of human nature is an extraordinarily painful task. A poster in a gay-owned store in New Orleans's French Quarter says it best: "Nothing is harder than not being yourself."

Bisexuality: An additional adaptation for young people struggling with issues of sexual orientation, which is actually a subset of the preceding category, is the group that identifies as bisexual during adolescence and later identifies as gay or lesbian when adults. While some are truly bisexual in their orientation and remain so throughout their lives, others self-identify as bisexual to either describe their sexual experimentation with both sexes, or because it is somehow less stigmatizing to be bisexual than gay or lesbian. For some young people bisexuality is a transition from heterosexuality to homosexuality; for others, bisexuality is a genuine sexual orientation. Robbie illustrates this point:

> When I was describing all of my problems during an intake interview, the director asked me if I was having problems in all of these places because I was gay? And that's when I got offended and I got up out of my seat and screamed at him, "I am not gay, I am bisexual! I have a girlfriend!" And he very calmly said, "Okay, you're bisexual, has that been the cause of some of your problems in the group home?" And I said "yes." I told him several months later that I was gay. I just wasn't ready to call myself gay at the interview.

Acceptance: "I can't conceive of the hidden life anymore, I don't think of it as a life. When you finally come out, there's a pain that stops, and you know it will never hurt like that again, no matter how much you lose or how bad you die" (Monette 1992:4).

The social ritual of coming out is the ending of hiding and secrecy and the beginning of acceptance.

For many young people, adolescence is a difficult and tumultuous period of development. Within limits and without much consequence or penalty, social and sexual experimentation is expected at this stage of life. A range of adolescent behavior is tolerated in the belief that young people can benefit from the opportunity to make their own decisions and live with their consequences, especially in light of the fact that they are at a time in their lives when they are not required to make lifelong commitments. In this interval of general confusion and experimentation, some young people will be locked in a struggle with questions of sexual orientation, and some will come to accept their gay or lesbian identity as a given.

Accepting one's identity is the third adaptive option which both Martin (1982) and Malyon (1982) allude to. Acceptance is reached once labeling or self-identification takes place, and a gay or lesbian positive sense of self is developed. At this juncture in time, an individual's sexual orientation is appropriately placed in perspective relative to his or her entire identity. Although acceptance is characterized as the refusal to invest all of one's energy in hiding, or in refusing to deny one's sexual identity, acceptance alone does not necessarily grant immediate access to a good fit.

Acceptance of oneself, a key element in this adaptive process, marked the end of the process of trying to change. Once young people accept their homosexual orientation and struggle to accept their own difference, many stop hiding. Wilma, a 20-year-old from New York, said:

> Yeah, I was eleven years old and we was upstate in an all-female group home and I knew I was never attracted to guys, I used to beat the guys up, I was attracted to the females and they used to always say "why do you beat up the guys and hang out with the females?" That was then, and I knew it then, but I tried to change it, and when I see I couldn't change it and that was my life, I accepted it.

Although many young people said they no longer pretended to have "changed," several noted that environmental forces lingered as hostile reminders that a good fit had not been fully achieved.

Most adolescents, including gays and lesbians, have a range of sexual and social experiences before they solidify their identity. Acceptance from others within an array of environmental contexts, as well as internal acceptance, was a key element. Tracey provides this experience of adaptation:

> It's just part of who I am. Don't get me wrong I had girlfriends left and right, but . . . there was no chemistry, but with a guy there was chemistry. . . at first it is a physical thing, but once you get into the person, you get to know the person and it starts to move to a mental and emotional plane. Straight people tend to think that people become gay because they are pressured into it. That's not true. People act like they can be forced to be gay, but if a person is gay it is because they are. People need to stop blaming other people. They need to just start accepting and stop saying it's wrong. Just accept it. We need self-assurance that it's not wrong, I mean people need to stop telling us we're wrong! I mean who are they to judge us.

Young gays and lesbians noted that part of the process of acceptance was the continual work they had to do to overcome negative environmental influences. Steven spoke about growing into his identity:

> I have always known that I was gay, but I needed time to grow. The group home system has always pointed out my sexuality in an indirect way saying: "He's going to have problems until he faces things in his life." I thought: "Who the fuck do they think they are judging me for being gay?" They very much saw it as a negative thing. I saw it as a negative thing too

at the time—I looked for a way out. I tried to date girls, I tried to sleep with a few, it just wasn't me. Now I'm more comfortable, but I still need time—it's like buying a new pair of shoes that are at first too big, you need time to grow into them.

Despite the continued lack of fit within the environment, some young people reported that they were liberated and proud of their gay/lesbian identity. Tamil was representative of many:

> Honey, let me tell you, when I finally came out and accepted who I was, there was no stopping me. When I came out, I was ready. I had been hiding for so long, feeling bad about who I was for such a long, long, time, that there was no way that I was ever gonna hide again. I was gay and I was proud. If people couldn't deal with me—fuck 'em. Ain't nobody, ever, gonna make me feel bad again. I struggled and I fought to be this person and damn it—I'm gonna live my life, my way!

As lesbian and gay young people strive to improve adolescent:environment "fit," many find, as a consequence to their environment's intolerance, that their internal sense of fit is not good. In response, they actively decide to adapt by choosing one of four options: they can hide; they can attempt to change themselves; they can opt to identify as bisexual as a transition toward a gay or lesbian identity; or they can accept their identity. In subsequent chapters, as we shall see, some opt for a fifth adaptation where they resolve to migrate to a new environment in the hope that they will find a cultural niche where they can be accepted and find a good fit (Germain 1985; Hartmann 1958).

Alert to the internal, environmental, and societal forces that have played on "people like them," these gays/lesbians presented illuminating analyses of the intersection of their own developmental processes within the context of the narratives from their own lives. They showed particular sensitivity to the contrast between internal sense of fit and the environmental perception of fit. Forcing oneself to fit into an identity where there is a poor fit is like wearing a left shoe on the right foot. It can be done, but it is uncomfortable. For others, they need time, as one young person put it, "to grow into their gayness." Recognizing the inherent maladaptive nature of, and psychic costs attributed to, hiding, most recalled that accepting themselves meant the end of this process and the end of trying to change themselves.

With few exceptions, these gay and lesbian people view themselves as resilient individuals who, having purposefully sidestepped hiding as heterosexuals, have had to grapple throughout their young lives with the challenge of balancing concealment and transformation to emerge as individuals who have accepted who they are. For many gays and lesbians interviewed for this study, the stress of negotiating a life within a hostile environment is directly related to the lack of family support. For many, this balancing act has required a high degree of resilience and self-awareness that proves, as we shall see, advantageous when you live as an outsider in your own family's home.

CHAPTER 2

| Searching for a Good Fit Within the Family System |

Families supply physical and emotional sustenance, connect individuals with their pasts, and provide a context within which people learn about the world, including the attitudes and mores of society (Berzon 1992). For the fifty-four gay/lesbian adolescents interviewed for this study, their reports suggest that the lack of family support for their identity generates a vacuum. Viewed within an ecological framework, growing up gay or lesbian in a heterosexual family is, by its very nature, a transactional process where the young person perceives a lack of fit. Having to keep one's sexual identity and affectional preferences secret from one's family creates an emotional and cognitive dissonance. Growing up within a family system where one cannot be or say who he or she truly is places young people in the continual position of having to negotiate life within an nonsupportive environment. Raul described the lack of nurturance received from his family:

> It's really difficult to be a gay teenager and to live at home. I was always on guard, always trying to hide who I was. I felt very isolated and really alone. My parents were very religious, so I knew that they would never accept me. On top of all that, we're Puerto Rican and you know Latin people have this real macho thing going on, so men are supposed to be into women, not other men.
>
> They were always saying awful things about gay and lesbian people and deep inside, even though I wasn't always sure, I knew that I was one of those people that they were always talking bad about. It made me feel terrible. In some ways, I always kinda thought that my parents knew about me, I mean they were always kinda dropping little hints, like "why don't you be more like your brothers," and "why can't you toughen up a bit," but in our family we just don't talk about those things, so nothing ever got discussed openly.

The Lack of Family Support

Dealing with a gay or lesbian child in a homophobic society creates family problems, provoking negative reactions even in families that are generally supportive and open. Many families develop effective coping devices to adjust to the child's disclosure, but other families are completely unprepared, and react in an unpredictable, negative manner.

Most young gays/lesbians are reared by heterosexual parents, without prior preparation for dealing with a child's homosexual orientation. Parents typically convey strong heterosexual messages to the effect that heterosexual relationships are the only valid and appropriate life goals. Some parents, particularly families with strong religious convictions, may openly condemn homosexuality, unaware that their own child is lesbian or gay. Although some families might not openly denounce homosexuality, "the absence of discussion sends a negative message" (Browning 1987:48). Such perceived negative biases make coming out to parents an extremely painful and stressful experience.

Disclosure to Families of Origin

Although burgeoning adolescent sexuality is seldom easy for any parent, most heterosexual adolescents grow up within a societal context that understands and accepts their behavior. As they become aware of their sexuality, most young people are supported by families who encourage and discuss dating and attraction to the opposite sex. In contrast, gay/lesbian adolescents lack such environmental nourishment because, by and large, they are void of familial and cultural role models. In communities of color, children are socialized to develop a pride in their culture. Children are taught adaptive behaviors for coping with oppression, discrimination, and racism. A moving example of such familial nourishment is related by the late Dr. Bessie Delany (Delany, Delany, and Hearth 1993:106), when she recalled this scene from her childhood:

> As a child every time I encountered prejudice . . . I would feel it down to my core. I was not a crying child, except when I was treated badly because of my race, . . . In those instances, I would go home and sit on my bed and weep and weep and weep, the tears streaming down my face.
>
> Now, Mama would come up and sit on the foot of my bed. She never said a word. She knew what I was feeling . . . Mama would just sit and look

at me while I cried, and it comforted me. I knew that she understood, and it was the most soothing salve.

In stark contrast, young gays and lesbians often cannot turn to family members to help them cope with environmental cruelty, as this story portrays:

> My mother was Jewish and my father was black. I got teased a lot. So when I came home from school, upset and crying that the kids in school had called me a bad name, I could talk to my Mom and she would understand because she too had been called those bad names. I could also talk to my Dad and he could soothe me because of his own experiences with racism. But who could I turn to when the kids called me a lezzie or a bull dyke? That was something that neither of my parents had experienced and something that I worked hard at trying to keep a secret.

While the professional literature focuses on parental reaction to disclosure by a child, empirical evidence (D'Augelli and Hershberger 1993:433) suggests that most young people do not first come out to their families. The majority of gays/lesbians (73%) disclosed first to a friend. Mothers were told first only 7% of the time; fathers, or both parents, were told first 1% of the time. Although the young people in the study confirmed that they did not first come out to their families, most expressed a strong desire to be open with their families, especially parents, but also siblings, grandparents, and other relatives.

Disclosure to Siblings

Jones (1984) suggests that sibling reactions are similar to those of parents, although he notes that there is generally no guilt or self-blame reported on the part of the sibling. Three transitional coping strategies are negotiated before a family member's homosexual identity is discovered or disclosed (Brown 1988).

First, analogous to the ecological tenet of migration, many of those interviewed sought to distance themselves, emotionally and/or geographically, from their families of origin, as 17-year-old Geoffery recalled:

> I became isolated. I stayed away from my family. I often wished I could move away from them to the city where there were other people like me and where no one knew me, but I was only sixteen years old. So instead, I became emotionally detached. I allowed myself to be absorbed by my art.

Second, others accede to the tacit family agreement that no one will discuss the personal life of the gay or lesbian. Julia notes:

> I went out with my girlfriends all the time. My family met them when they came to call for me, but we all had an unspoken agreement that we wouldn't discuss it.

Third involves disclosing to a family member. Some young people, like Albert, disclosed to family members incrementally, one at a time, with the emotionally closest members being told first, with the understanding that the individual would not tell other family members.

> When I finally decided that it was time to come out I first told my sister whom I am closest to in my family. I kinda knew that no matter what I told her that she would not reject me, so I figured that I would test the waters with her. When I told her that I was gay, she said "hey, you're my brother and I love you no matter what." That made me feel great and then when I told my mother about five months later it was easier. When I told my mother, I told her that I had already told my sister and that she could talk to her if she wanted to talk to someone about this. I think that helped her too.

Sometimes, however, siblings were not empathetic and trustworthy confidants, as Alejandro illustrates:

> In my case, I didn't have a choice about whether or not to come out to my parents because my sister outed me. I had told her that I was gay a few months before and she thought that I needed help to tell my parents, so she just took it upon herself to tell them for me. I guess she was trying to help, but I was really not ready to tell them I was gay. But once it happened, I had no choice. When they asked if I was, I told them yes.

Sadly, some parents believe that their gay or lesbian child might molest a younger sibling or another child in the home. Several excerpts excerpts illustrate this point:

> If parents are not educated, then they might think that their gay kid is gonna try to influence a younger sibling to be gay or maybe they might think that the gay child might molest the younger sibling. You never know . . . I mean if parents don't know about gay people, and most of

them don't, they might believe all of this stuff. I know that's how it was for me . . . I have a younger brother and I was always afraid that if I came out to my mother that she would think that maybe I might molest him—it put a lot of stress on me.

They didn't want me to be around their biological kids. I mean they were two years old! Who would want them? They thought that I was going to do something to them. It was a family group home—I guess they thought I'd hurt one of them, you know pull a 288 (a child molestation petition) on one of them.

It hurt me. Because I'm gay doesn't mean, I'm going to molest a child. I mean my uncle was always trying to protect his daughter as if I was going to molest her or something. I wasn't interested in her. It really hurt me that he felt that I might do that.

Disclosure to Other Relatives

The family of origin does not consist solely of parents and siblings. In many cases, however, families are vested in "keeping their family business" within their immediate families. At disclosure, parents may ask the young person not to disclose to other members of the larger family system. Albert and José made comments which illustrate this point:

It's like okay you told us, but don't tell anyone else in the family. Don't tell Aunt Laverne and don't tell your grandparents because they have weak hearts—but you know, grandparents are really more understanding sometimes because they are older and because they've been around longer.

Whenever my relatives visit from the Dominican Republic, my mother always warns me not to talk about being gay. She always assures me that it's not because she can't accept it, but, as she says, "you know those people, they would never understand and then they'd all go back to La Capital and tell everyone." When I assure her that I don't care and tell her that I'm out to everyone, she then says, "could you please just do this for me?" I usually agree, but it makes me feel like I'm always having to go back in the closet to please my family. I don't like that part of it.

Young people who participated in the study reported that regardless of how (disclosure or discovery) they came out to their families, when a family member of a family comes out, the entire family system comes out (DeVine 1984). In this process a family system advances through five states of perception and recognition of a family member's gay or lesbian identity: tacit awareness, response, adaptation, settlement, and amalgamation.

In *tacit awareness*, a gay or lesbian identity is surmised because of behavioral and communication differences. The following quotation by the mother of a gay young man (Tuerk 1995), obtained from the literature, clearly resonates with one mother's recollection of sensing her son's differentness:

> We noticed early that Joshua was different. He was not a rough-and-tumble, fearless boy with an ardent interest in matchbox cars and balls, who skinned his knees climbing trees or pretended to be a six-gun-wielding cowboy. He was timid and gentle and liked nothing better than playing house and make-believe games with the girls in the neighborhood. "He's artistic," I told myself, uneasy with the other word that was running through my head: "effeminate" . . . Like many parents, I fell prey to fears that my son's differences meant he would grow up to be *one of them*, a homosexual (Tuerk 1995: 18).

Other published literature (Borhek 1979, 1988; Dew 1994; Fairchild and Hayward 1989; Griffin, Wirth, and Wirth 1986) written by the parents of gays/lesbians and more recently Internet sites (http://www.pflag.org) have made similar observations.

Many of the young people's comments suggested that mothers seem to have a greater awareness of a child's sexual orientation than do fathers. Philip illustrates this point:

> I think that Moms always know. Dads don't. I guess if you're really effeminate or something, they could guess. Yeah, Moms usually know, they sense that something is different, they always know—they might not make the connection with homosexuality, but as you get older they know. Moms obviously want the best for their kids, but they keep this thought in the back of their head—but it's always there. I think that a lot of them think that this is how you are now as a young kid, but that it will change as you hit puberty and meet girls and all. With Dads it's more of the things that they just don't know. They see a boy playing with a Barbie doll and they say, "oh, no," so they take it away and give them a toy truck instead. With dads it's like a thing that they think they can guide you out of it—they think of being different as like a temporary moment of insanity. I don't think they really have any idea that their kid is gay or lesbian. Moms know, they may be

oblivious to the idea—but they know. That's why if you come out they're shocked because they have pushed it so far back.

Response is characterized by "discovery" or disclosure and is usually experienced as a crisis situation for the family system. Albert's recollection best illustrates this point:

> At first, like most kids, I was not out to my family, I mean I knew I was different, but I didn't realize that it meant that I was gay. When I started to meet people, and guys would call my house, my mother would say "Who are these guys calling, are they gay? They sound gay!" At that point, all eyes are upon you, stuff like that makes people focus on you. It's like being hawked [watched] over twenty-four hours a day, seven days a week. Everybody is paying attention because you're watched all the time. Parents can become very restrictive, they change your curfew, they get stricter—it's like you get treated like you have an illness—like you're an invalid, like you're not right.

In *adaptation* parents urge a son or daughter either to change a gay or lesbian orientation or encourage keeping that identity a secret—thus maintaining the family's reputation and respectability. Maurice captured the essence of adaptation with this example:

> When I finally sat down and had "the talk" with my mother she cried, and cried. She first tried to get me to agree to go to see a psychologist to see if I could change. When I told her that I had been in therapy for two years and that I was not interested in changing, she was shocked. I told her that I felt good about who I was. Then she got really worried that I might tell other people, you know, the neighbors, other relatives. She said, "If that's your lifestyle fine, but please don't go around and announce it to everybody." It was really hard, I wished that she had been able to be more supportive of me.

Settlement is that state where the family mourns the loss of the fantasized heterosexual role for the child and dispels negatives myths about homosexuality. Family support can be a great encouragement, as it was for Maura:

> After a few months, my Mom got used to the idea that I was a lesbian and said that she wanted to go to P-FLAG (Parents and Friends of Lesbians and Gays). I was so happy. She really got into going to meeting and learning

more about people who were gay and lesbian. I think that it helped her that there were other parents who shared her experiences. Now, she's one of my biggest advocates.

In *amalgamation*, the final state, the role for the son or daughter and new behaviors for dealing with gay/lesbian identity are enacted. Patrick corroborated this association:

When I first came out, it was hard for my parents, they cried and seemed stunned. After a few months, they seemed to deal with things better. They began to ask me questions, they told me that no matter what, that they loved me. Things are now pretty normal—my being gay is not an issue— it's just part of who I am.

When a family member comes out, there are a multitude of responses. At one end of the continuum is acceptance, but rarely, if ever, is this announcement celebrated. Instead, the coming-out announcement is often met with negative responses ranging from mild disapproval to complete nonacceptance and dissociation. These responses cause considerable stress and pain for the lesbian and gay person, as José recalls:

When I told my parents I was gay, my father just stared at me and my mother just cried. It was really painful. When I realized that my own family couldn't accept me, my own flesh and blood, I thought, "Why should I expect the rest of society to cut me any slack. I felt hopeless, disillusioned, and worthless. My own family . . . how could they do that to me, be so cold, so uncaring, it was as if they were saying they didn't care if I lived or died. I don't think I'll ever get over that."

Parental Reactions to Disclosure

Parental perceptions of a gay/lesbian identity of a son or daughter take in a range of disapproving reactions. The first is that most parents, unfamiliar with homosexuality, apply their negative conceptions to their own offspring. Initial parental reactions to disclosure can include denying the reality of that sexual orientation; ignoring the issue or treating disclosure with silence; trying to change the person; or breaking contact with their children. Parental perceptions are further exacerbated by powerful feelings of guilt and failure. Add to these that one of the big-gest problems for families with a gay or lesbian family member is embarrassment.

"It's Just a Phase"

My family always had their suspicions, but they thought it was just a phase.

Many parents, unsure of how to process a son's or daughter's attraction to same-gendered individuals, initially hope that it represents a transient ado-lescent phase of development. Although same-gender sexual behavior alone does not predispose one toward a homosexual orientation, most families have difficulty believing that some young people could be considered gay or lesbian before they reach adulthood. As such, the possibility of adolescent homosexuality was dismissed. Malyon (1981:324), notes that "many . . . have regarded all reports of homosexual fantasy or behavior as an indica-tion of "sexual identity confusion" and viewed any type of same-sex eroti-cism as no more than a transient developmental phenomenon." Reassuring a youngster that his/her feelings are "just a phase" and that such feelings do not indicate the existence of a fixed homosexual orientation is often the tra-ditional parental standard response for an adolescent expressing same-gen-dered sexual affection. Such a standard response sends the message to the young person that to be lesbian or gay is an undesirable and inferior sexu-al orientation, as Treg's observation implies:

> Well, I was in junior high when I first knew, but I just always seemed dif-ferent. You don't even know how to explain it, you don't know if it's a phase or whatever. But I knew. I mean how do you come up to you parent and tell 'em you're gay, so when I did, Mama looked at me and said "That's just a stage you're going through." She tried to send me to a psychiatrist and tried to find out what was wrong, but it didn't help. I eventually just accepted that I was gay.

"We Never Talked About It"

Some families do not openly denounce homosexuality, but simply avoid any and all discussion about the topic, as Patrick suggests:

> I knew that I was gay when I was about five and I think my mother was aware of it, but she just never commented on it. She commented on it one

time, but it wasn't, it wasn't positive or negative, she said, "if that's what you want to do, just be careful," and I felt, kind of strange, I knew what she was talking about but I just didn't say anything. She said, "if that's what you want to do, you know, just be safe and be careful." But I didn't really, at that time, I didn't really say much about it. I didn't say much either.

Familial silence, as described by Trevor, had a profound impact:

Once you're out, you can't jump back in. If you come out, you can't erase it. A lot of times after you're out it's like let's just go on with things the way they were before—let's not talk about it. I mean what am I gonna say "Hey, Mom, I met this great guy." I mean we just don't talk about it—I think, families think if they don't talk about it, then it will go away—like a bad dream. That part is hard, because if I'm out with everyone, I also want to be out to my family. But families just don't want to hear about it—they say "Tell me about school," "Tell me about your job—I don't want to hear about your gay lifestyle." It's sad, I wanted to share my life with my family, but they're always saying "You don't have to shove it in our faces—couldn't you just keep it to yourself!" "No, you're my family—this is me—this is who I am."

Remee spoke about the effects that silence had on her:

It's really difficult to be a lesbian teenager and to live at home. My Mom and I never talk about the fact that I'm a lesbian. Sometimes the silence really gets to me.

Jason's comments suggest that he had internalized his family's message:

I think if they knew that they wouldn't have anything to do with me. They don't allow that in their family. They're just against gays.

"You've Got to Change"

Some families, like Maria's, react to disclosure with a demand for therapy to "change."

Me and my mother, we just couldn't get along. I, I knew at that time, at sixteen I knew I was gay, I knew before that, but at sixteen that's when I made up my mind to it . . . I knew at twelve or thirteen, but at twelve or thirteen, I mean, how do you come up to your parent and tell em that you are gay, so when I did, Mama looked at me and said "That's just a stage you're going through because you acting up in school" and stuff like that—there's something more to it. She tried to send me to a psychiatrist and tried to find out what was wrong, to try and change me. But I knew even back then, that there was no way to change me and after a while she saw that I couldn't be changed either.

Impact of Race, Culture, and Religion

Race, culture, and religion have a significant impact on the development of individual attitudes about a social phenomenon. Parents' racial, cultural, and religious biases also play a pivotal role in the development of negative attitudes toward gay and lesbian youth.

Although antigay/antilesbian hostility is present in all cultures (Annin 1990), adults from Caribbean countries were singled out by the adolescents in this study as particularly having negative attitudes toward gays and lesbians. Those participants from Trinidad, Jamaica, the Dominican Republic, and Puerto Rico described the deeply ingrained negative attitudes about their identity held by family members who declared that their island cultures proudly and loudly proclaimed themselves to be antigay and antilesbian. These reports were graphically illustrated in the experiences of young people with Jamaican parents or staff members. Alex illustrates this point in a graphic manner:

> Well, I got into it with my mother. She wouldn't accept my sexuality. She found men's and women's magazines in my room, in my box, and she beat me, cursed at me, and kept asking me, "Why do you want to be gay? Why do you want to be a homo? Why do you want to be a faggot? Don't you want a family and don't you want to make me a proud mother?" I said I didn't want a family and I didn't want a wife and she slapped me across the face. Then she gave an extension cord to my stepfather and he took over and then started beating me. He's Jamaican and they don't like gay people, he beat for me about ten or fifteen minutes, he was always beating me and I just got sick of it.

Carl, a Jamaican-born youth, connected Jamaican bias against gays and lesbians with religion:

> The Jamaican culture is antihomosexual; if you lived there and were gay, you'd be dead. You'd have to hide yourself especially from the older peo-

ple. The religion always says that it has to be a man and a woman so most of them are wrapped up in that and they can't accept difference and it's a sin if you are different.

Tina, who is Trinidadian, said similar things about Trinidad's attitudes toward gays and lesbians:

There was no family network for support. I am Trinidadian and it was very, very taboo. We are a very antilesbian and antigay culture. There was no connection and no networking from my family. I was told that I was not able to go to our community that way.

Latinos, particularly those from Caribbean countries, were also identified as a group that had trouble dealing with homosexuality. Raul, himself from Puerto Rico, observed:

I think the Puerto Ricans, Dominicans, and all Latino groups have a big problem with homosexuals. I mean, there's a big problem in our culture if you are gay or lesbian. I mean if you're homosexual, you're a disgrace to your family, it's like being the lowest of the low, it's like being a drug addict.

Several Latino young people suggested that being gay or lesbian was something that families may have known, but agreed not to talk about. Robbie, a native of Puerto Rico, best captured this tension with the following account:

My family knows, but we don't talk about it. You know Puerto Rican families, they have all this shit going on, but we just don't openly discuss it.

The Nicaraguan youths I interviewed did not mention the bias of their homelands.

Some families, particularly families with strong religious convictions, may openly condemn homosexuality, unaware that their own offspring is lesbian or gay. Blumenfeld and Raymond (1988) note that families with strong religious convictions often support their religious views even against a family member. Parents' personal biases, particularly cultural or religious biases that view homosexuality negatively, can make "coming out" a painful experience.

Young African Americans, particularly those reared in the southern part of the United States, noted that their families had strong connections to their churches. These African Americans connected disapproval of gays and lesbians to religion as opposed to race.

Several noted that their church leaders taught them to view homosexuality as sinful, morally offensive, and unforgivable. Such religious responses are more likely to be related to fundamentalist Christianity in general than to African-American churches in particular. One African American, Sharice, who came from a fundamentalist Christian background, made this personal observation:

> I guess cause they weren't open-minded, more religious people had a harder time. My grandmother took me to the preacher to ask him to pray for me so the devil wouldn't take over me. I had the whole church praying for me. They told me it was an abomination. The Christian part of my family had a real hard time with me being a lesbian.

Many family members were so intolerant that they threatened a gay/lesbian family member with eternal damnation, as these two noted:

> My family said, it's a sin you'll go to hell.

> My family dealt with it real bad. My dad was upset, my aunts said I'd go to hell. I don't know . . . it was hard.

Still another young man elaborated on his familial experience with religious intolerance for his identity:

> Everybody in the family knew that I was gay. The only person that didn't agree with me being gay was my mother, of course. Everyone else that I thought was not going agree, did agree. My mother said that she hated me and to this very day she tells me that it is against God's will and it's against his proposition and when the day comes for him to take over the world again you're going to suffer and I don't want you to suffer cause you're my son, my oldest son, and I don't want anything to happen to you, you know. And I will be telling her, Mommy I know, I understand but this is something that I am and you know, I believe if there's a way that God wants to help me or whatever, that it's not right, then he will help me, but right now I don't think that this is actually bothering God because I believe that back in the Roman days things like this used to happen and if it's a sin that I'm sorry and to this very day she yaps at me about it when I come to her house.

Acceptance

If lesbians or gays had early, positive experiences when discussing other difficult issues with their families, they may choose to come out to their parents. Parental reaction to such a disclosure can be a positive experience, increasing the level of intimacy and honesty with parents, as it was with Sharte:

> My Mom always knew. When we finally sat down and "had the talk" and I said "Mom, I have to talk to you," she said, "I know, you're gay, right?" I was so relieved. I had heard from so many of my friends how terrible their experiences were and even though we have always had a positive relationship, I was scared that she would not be able to deal with me being gay and it would ruin everything.

Prior positive contact with gay or lesbian people (kin, friends, neighbors) seemed to help parents accept their youngster's sexual orientation. This was the case for Sharte:

> My mother told me, she said, "You are a faggot." What happened was my mother and I was having this big discussion, I was thirteen years old at the time and we was in the kitchen and I'll never forget, I was smoking a cigarette and she said, "Is there anything you want to tell me?" And I said, "No, there is nothing, what do you want to know?" And she said "Well, there is something I want to tell you." And I said, "What can you tell me that I don't already know about myself?" And she said, "You's just gonna grow up to be a little faggot." And I said, "Oh, my God!" I knew I always liked boys, I always knew that so it wasn't like a big shock to stress out my life, I mean I always liked boys, but I just never let it show . . . Well, maybe I did, maybe I did let it show, I mean I did dress in tight clothes at that time, but I just thought that was me, I just thought that was natural, it was nature, I didn't think anything else. But my mother dealt with it, I mean she had sisters that was gay, and her nieces and her nephews, so it wasn't like I was the only one, she just took it hard because I was her first child. Which turned out to be bad, me being the oldest and all.

Coming Out Versus Being Found Out

In some cases, young gays and lesbians do not have the opportunity to voluntarily disclose their sexual identity before family members "discover" their "secret." Albert told of his experience with being "found out:"

When a family member finds out, it's easier—they look for signs, they probably had an idea to begin with—the whole idea was in their mind. If a family member finds you out, they can either confront you or keep it a secret. I know in my case, my Mom would go through my stuff, but she wouldn't say anything. I'd come home and find all of my *Out* magazines in the garbage. She would throw them all away, as if doing that would somehow magically change me. Her way of dealing with it was just to pretend that they were never there. She would never bring it up, and we would never talk about it.

If you're found out, it's a violation—I mean you didn't decide. Lots of times you have to lie—like I did—you have to. You have to defend yourself and either continue lying or admit it. It's a very scary thing to be found out—it's nauseating, you think: "Oh, no! What the hell am I gonna do now?" The first thing that comes to mind is panic—oh shit, oh shit, oh shit, oh shit! It's like being caught red-handed, it's like the cops are right there and you're caught. It's frightening, it's like death knocking on your door—I mean it's that dramatic, it's that frightening. I didn't want my family to know I was gay. I was ashamed, I mean how was I going to deal with being openly gay? At the point I was caught I thought it was bad to be gay. I didn't want to confess to it. I was not prepared.

When you come out, though, it's different—it's like POOF! I mean it's a panic state, it's like what the fuck is this? There can be dead silence or a riot. It's harder for the gay child when they come out. But I guess it's the same thing for the parent when the child decides to come out, they are not prepared.

Parental Guilt and Embarrassment

Some parents erroneously blame themselves for their role modeling in determining the child's sexual orientation. "What did I do wrong?" is a common self-blaming refrain. Parents also worry about being blamed by others in the community. As previously stated, when a member of the family comes out, the entire family system is forced to come out as well (De Vine 1984). Albert again relates this detailed account of his story:

> Being a gay teenager is mixed up with teenage angst. You know—no one understands me because I am a teenager—but it's worse because no one understands me because I'm gay. I mean as difficult as it to deal with this whole teenage thing, it's worse being a teenager who is gay.
>
> I think parents feel—"I don't know my kid." Parents feel guilt—"it's my fault." It brings a big gap between parents and their child. The child feels

guilty because they think, of, "No I'm to blame for this whole thing!" Being gay or lesbian changes a lot of things for a family.

For some parents, like Maura's and like Remee's, embarrassment is a primary reaction:

> Everybody knows, my mother had a big problem with it though, she thinks I'm into dressing like a man, and it bothers her.

> My mom doesn't talk to me. I don't have a home anymore. My sister is all right, but the rest are not. My mom has a difficult time with me being a lesbian. Once we went to Popeye's [a take-out chicken shop] and a girl was flirting with me and my mom got very upset and said I was never to do that again.

The Harsh Realities a Poor Fit

We have seen how some parents respond with verbal harassment or physical abuse when they find out about a son's or daughter's homosexuality. Disclosure of sexual orientation to a parent or "discovery" can also lead to expulsion from the home:, as with Richard, José, and Tamil: Richard's narrative:

> When my mother found out that I was gay (she overheard a conversation that I was having with my boyfriend on the telephone) she just flew into this wild rage. She started screaming that she wasn't having THAT in her house and then started to throw things at me. I was so shocked. I started to scream back at her and then she slapped me across the face screaming like a wild-woman that I should leave the house immediately. I left because I had to, but I was completely unprepared for her to act that way.

José's:

> One day my father heard me talking on the telephone to a guy who I had met. When I got off the phone he just went crazy on me, he started slapping me and saying that he didn't raise me to be no faggot. He told me to get the hell out of his house and literally threw me out the front door. I was devastated. I didn't know where to go, I had no place to go. I walked the streets for a long time and then I called and a friend who let me stay at his house. My friend told me about a shelter for young people and I went there. They helped me to get into a group home and that's where I am now.

I've tried to call my parents, I would really like to talk to them, but they won't take my calls.

Tamil's:

I was having a lot of problems at home with my mother. She has a real hard time with me being gay. We fought about a lot of things. One day when I came home from school she had all of my things packed in black plastic garbage bags and told me to get the fuck out. I had no place to go, but I had to leave.

Physically abusive responses, in some cases, came from families that already seemed to have been experiencing a great deal of life stress. Tony's experience best captures this phenomenon:

If the reaction is terrible then obviously you regret coming out. If everything explodes, then I guess some kids run away. If it's an abusive family, they will throw it in your face. It can be used against you—if there's a fight they say: "first you told us that you're gay, now this." It can be used to manipulate. It's a parent's worst nightmare for their child to be gay. After realizing that it's not going to get better, some kids say, "fuck this—I'm leaving." In some cases there might be a beating involved—especially if the father feels "I'll make a man of you yet. This is what you get for hurting your mother like you did."

A family's inability to talk about or accept a gay/lesbian sexual orientation causes some adolescents, like Brenda, to leave their homes voluntarily, to seek out a niche with a better fit.

I didn't tell my Mom that I was a lesbian. I just wasn't sure that I could and even if I did, I wasn't sure how she would react, so I just started staying out late, staying at a friend's houses, you know, kinda distancing myself from her and then eventually I just moved in with a friend. We still talk, and sometimes I visit her, but I just can't live there anymore.

Prematurely leaving one's family separates one from one's family and requires the ultimate assumption of adult responsibilities and social roles (Mallon 1994a; Malyon 1981). Homelessness, foster care placement, or survival prostitution are frequent consequences of leaving home at a young age, as it was for this woman:

When I got thrown out of my Mom's apartment, I wasn't ready to live on my own. I didn't even know where to go. But I didn't have a choice, she just packed my things and showed me the door. After going from sofa to sofa staying at friends' houses, I finally got hooked up to foster care.

When families were accepting, young people remained in their homes and renegotiated their newly configured lives within the context of their family system. When the fit was poor, as it was for most of those interviewed, many either opted to live in silence or left home to seek out a more affirming environment.

Gays and lesbians need to be part of their families as much as any young people. Given the stigmatizing status that homosexuality still holds for many in society, the family is one place where gays/lesbians most need to feel accepted. Most hope that their families, those who know them best, those who are responsible for guiding and nurturing them through life, will realize that they are the same persons they have always been, but many of the fifty-four found quite the opposite, and left their homes to search for a better fit, a fit that many assumed might be found in an out-of-home-care setting.

CHAPTER 3

| Searching for a Good Fit Within an | Out-of-Home-Care Setting

The Placement Experience

Young people living apart from their families have to learn to adapt to a new and unfamiliar environment. Out-of-home-care settings are generally not warm and homelike. In his classic work on the social system of a group of young boys in a cottage environment, Polsky (1962) points out that young people placed in group care learn quickly that in order to survive, they must be aware of the culture of the environment and play by its rules. In out-of-home-care settings, agency administrators may ordain the guidelines for care, but individual staff members, usually child care workers and social workers, set the tone and interpret the cultural norms of the setting. These staff members have been sanctioned by their agency's administrators to exert control and authority over the young people placed in their care and to insure the smooth operation of the social system. Sexuality of any type in group care is often a taboo subject and is almost never openly discussed.

Young people placed in group care are routinely categorized according to age, but individually, each one comes into placement for a variety of reasons. Some are troubled, others are delinquent, and many simply have no families available to care for them. An informal system of rules and norms is generally put in place by the residents who live in the group or foster home. A pecking order (Polsky 1962:7–49) ranging from strongest to weakest is operative and is a powerful force to contend with. Ranking (in contemporary inner city terms this is now known as "snapping on people"), scapegoating, and forming of subgroups and cliques are all part of the social structure of group living. Most gays and lesbians in this study reported that they were on the bottom rungs of this social ladder.

Gays and lesbians have historically been identified as the group care system's scapegoats—the "queers"—the constituents with the lowest status.

Participation in any activity of a same-gender sexual nature immediately consigns one to a second-rate level. Confirming this conceptualizing of group care culture, Polsky (1962:85) notes: "The big men and the con-artists, on the one hand, the scapegoats and the queers, on the other, constitute the extremes of the cottage role system continuum of peer group behavior in the cottage." These gays and lesbians live with the triple threat of first being marginalized by society, second, being misunderstood by their own families, and then finally being placed away from their family in a group/foster home or campus setting.

Multiple Placements

Moving from one's family to an out-of-home-care setting is stressful in and of itself, but moving subsequently from one placement to another, a theme heretofore noted as a major difficulty in out-of-home care (Fanshel 1982; Fanshel and Shinn 1978; Maas and Engler 1959), overwhelms any sense of permanence. The constant challenge of adapting to a new environment arouses anxiety and unsettledness. Unlike other adolescents in out-of-home care who move from setting to setting because of behavioral problems, those interviewed for this study reported that it was their sexual orientation itself that led to multiple and unstable placements. They reported experiencing unstable placements for various reasons: they were not accepted by staff because staff had difficulties dealing with their sexual orientation; they felt unsafe because of their sexual orientation and either awoled from the placement for their own safety or requested replacement; they were perceived as a management problem by staff because they were open about their sexual orientation; and they were not accepted by peers because of their sexual orientation. Maura's narrative is illustrative:

> I couldn't live at home with my mother, because she couldn't deal with the fact that I was a dyke. So, let me give you the sequence: I currently live at the Jane Residence, which is a part of St. Peter's. But I was first placed in a diagnostic center, the Children's Center. But I left there after about ten minutes when I could tell that they couldn't deal with my orientation. I awoled from there and stayed at my grandmother's house. They didn't say anything about me being a lesbian but it was damn obvious that they had a problem with me. If I felt that they couldn't deal with me, I just

awoled, I mean my feeling was, I couldn't live at home because my mother couldn't deal with it, and if the staff in the group home can't deal with
it either, then why bother sticking around? After that I went back to my
mother, then to Grand Street Group Home and then to John Street Group
home, which is another of St. Peter's group homes, then to where I am
now, Community House.

Because staff reject their orientation many gay/lesbian youngsters are
"gotten rid of" by an agency and have had multiple placements or replace-
ments in all levels of care. Wilem's account represents many:

> I have had so many placements, I can't even remember. Too many to re-
> member, all of those overnights . . . a lot of places. I was fourteen when I
> went to my first one, I've been to lots of them, but I kept running away be-
> cause I just couldn't live there. I even was running away from home because
> I didn't want anyone to know that I was gay. The best was The Meadows
> and the worst was Mount Laurel. It wasn't horrible but it still wasn't the
> best place to be. I stood it at The Partnership for a while because I met some
> gays there that I knew from outside, so we hung out together and they
> showed me the ropes and we hung out together.

Within an ecological perspective, these findings suggest that the majority of the gays and lesbians in this study were continuously negotiating
new environments, many of which were inhospitable and unable to provide them with the nutrients necessary for healthy growth because of their
sexual orientation. The unfolding of a poor fit, one solely because of sexual orientation (a central element in these young people's developmental
process and family systems), was also dominant in the data.

Replacement and Feelings of Rejection

Feeling that they were not welcome in care, and feeling isolated in many
of the placements where they were reluctantly accepted, the majority of
the group had strong negative reactions to their out-of-home-care placements. Many were quite impassioned about their maltreatment in these
settings, as Wilem illustrates:

> How was I treated? You mean the way we were treated? It sucks, it sucks.
> I mean I wouldn't want to go back to one. It's hard enough being in a situ-
> ation when you are away from your family and then having somebody else
> put you down . . . I mean, it's just not fair.

Some reported that they left their placement when they felt they were not welcome. Maura recalled this experience vividly:

> As soon as I get discriminated against, I leave. I mean when I was on a psychiatric ward they were trying to give me aversion therapy and I mean they were supposed to help me with my depression, not by telling me that I'm wrong. Where I am now, they are fine, but in other places definitely there were problems. I mean when I was in Lakewood, they were giving me my own room because I was gay to keep the other kids away from me. It's the kids and the staff that treat you differently.

Young people who left placements frequently became lost in the system as their multiple placements caused them to feel a sense of impermanence and drift (Maas and Engler 1959).

Positive Experiences

Only a small number of young people (n=5) reported that their experiences in out-of-home care were highly positive. Celine, from Toronto, best represents this viewpoint:

> Wherever you go, you know you're going to hear positive and negative. My experience was mostly positive. Like before I told anyone I had gained everyone's respect anyway and knew everyone at the point in time, so there were no problems really. In fact my friend, the one I was closest to, she was the last one to find out and we were in the same room.

Those interviewed reported that finding a good fit within an out-of-home placement seemed to be closely linked to the presence of three key factors: staff who were understanding and responsive to their needs; peers who were like them or who were able to deal with personal difference; and visible signs and symbols that demonstrated acceptance and supplied indications that the milieu was a safe environment. Paula made this comment:

> All the staff are really gay positive, you know, lesbian positive and they are really easy to talk to. In fact a lot of the staff are gay and it was kind of funny because that's where I really came out, when I was there and I found it so easy. Everybody in the house knew and nobody cared, we all got along and it was just fun all the time. We were always talking about these women

and those women and just laughing all the time —it was comfortable because I was not the only one. From the moment that I walked in the door
and saw that poster with the pink triangle that sent a clear message to me
that this place was okay.

Staff

Gay and lesbian staff members were considered to have special advantages in promoting a positive sense of fit between gay and lesbian young
people and their out-of-home environments. All young people need positive role models to guide them in their journey toward adulthood. The
presence of gay or lesbian staff was a powerful and positive force in finding a good fit, as suggested by Ralph, from New York:

> There were gay staff like crazy in the agencies I lived in. It helps to have a
> positive influence, it's like I'm gay and I can help you. Having a straight per-
> son work with a gay counselor is also good because they can then see that
> it's ok that there is nothing strange or wrong with them, they help.

Katrina, from Toronto, asserted that gay or lesbian staff members were
supportive and helpful:

> All four of the staff that were lesbians, they all said to me, "If you have any
> questions or anything, any concerns, you need to know information about
> this or that and the other thing, sex or whatever, you know," they all said,
> "feel free to come to me anytime—I'll always make time for you."

Patrick, from Los Angeles, attested to this, noting that gay-identified staff
had a higher level of comfort in working with gay or lesbian young people:

> Gay staff know more, they feel comfortable with you and they are not em-
> barrassed about it or anything like that.

Paula recalled how she initially went to speak with a heterosexually oriented woman who ultimately referred her to a lesbian worker because she
was perceived as more skilled at working with Paula:

> I had gone to one of the staff who wasn't lesbian and she didn't know too
> much, you know how to give me any counseling at all, so you know she
> said that I should talk to Pat [an openly lesbian staff member]. Pat knew
> why I wanted to talk to her. She just kind of laid it all out on the table and
> said, boom, boom, boom, here you go.

Just as young gays/lesbians were not always identifiable to professionals, gay and lesbian staff members were not always identifiable to the young people I interviewed. Nonetheless, some of them tacitly understood some staff to be gay or lesbian. They felt that gay and lesbian staff transmitted more subtle cues, some of which could be detected only by what is known in the gay and lesbian community as "gaydar" (Grunson 1993; Musto and Bright 1993), defined as the unique ability for gays/lesbians to recognize other gays/lesbians. Noting these phenomena, Miguel said:

> Some of the staff were not open about their sexual orientation either. But I could always tell the ones who were gay or lesbian. I don't know how to describe it, it's just something that you sense about them. Even though they weren't out, most of them were cool.

In settings where the staff members were not open about their sexual identity, most of the study group recalled that they lent their support nonetheless. The comments of Shawn and José were typical:

> I always thought that Pam was gay, she never told me or anything, I guess she couldn't because if the other kids found out it would be gossip and all that, but, I always thought she was gay and she was really great, she talked to me and showed me that she understood.

> The only person who talked to me was one counselor, who I figured out later was gay himself. He was the only one I talked to about being gay and once in a while one of the other workers would because their supervisors were there.

Many young people felt that empathy of the worker (Hepworth and Larson 1993; Raines 1990), rather than their sexual orientation, helped to facilitate a good fit between them and their placement environment. Underscoring this point, Tracey said:

> Well, I mean to me, it really doesn't matter if they are gay or lesbian or straight, as long as they are open, you know. I probably would feel more comfortable with a gay or lesbian staff, but I've also dealt with the straight staff who are real open people and they are willing to learn about this so that they don't have the wrong perceptions. I am just open with people that are just open. They have no barriers within them.

Like all young people in out-of-home care, gays and lesbians responded best to staff who were empathetic, caring, and responsive to their needs, as Tracey continued:

> The staff at Horizon House was good because one of them was gay and I got along with her real good, and the staff at The Center is good, they don't care, they accept me for who I am, who I am is who I am as far as they are concerned.

Maurice identified the most exceptional staff as those who respected gay and lesbian young people:

> The best staff are those that respect you for who you are, rather than judge you for what you do. They don't have to be gay, they don't have to be straight, they just have to listen without judging. People who are nasty and have nasty attitudes make me feel uncomfortable, you know the people who just work for the money, not to help kids.

Steven identified the staff who listened as the most responsive, as evidenced by this vivid recollection:

> The staffs here sit and listen, try to understand you, you know if you do something wrong they are going say—"hey, that was wrong." They don't tell you exactly what to do, they just make suggestions, they are very suggestive. I can talk to people here and sometimes I don't even have to tell them they'll know, like I'll come in smiling and they'll say—"who's the new guy?" It's like they know and it feels good. Like last night I was coming upstairs and a staff supervisor who is female said "Hi!" I was smiling like crazy and she said "Are you all right?" And I said "Yeah, I'm all right" and I went upstairs and she said "Be careful now, 'cause love hurts you know," and I went upstairs.

> If I was ever to bring that to another group home, the staff would give me an ugly face and say "Don't tell me about that, I don't really want to hear it!" That was always the dominate response, they didn't want to hear about it. They didn't want to deal with it. I could tell that they weren't so fond of homosexuals and I don't think they wanted to get to know any homosexuals 'cause they looked down on them. To me it doesn't matter if staffs are gay or lesbian or straight, as long as they are open. I would probably feel more comfortable with a gay or lesbian staff, but I have also dealt with the straight staff who are real open people and they are willing to learn about

this so they don't have the wrong perceptions. I am just open with people that are just open. My social worker is straight and my therapist is straight too, I never thought about that, that's weird.

Child welfare professionals, ideally, assume the role of parent for a young person in out-of-home care. Staff members are expected to play an important nurturing role. Those staff members who affirmed the identity of young people, regardless of their own sexual orientation, were viewed by young people as the most valuable resources of all. Several of those interviewed identified the inestimable value of these individuals:

There were one or two staff members there though that I could talk to and they made it all right. Liz was one of them, I loved her, I think I am going to invite her to my graduation. I always thought she was gay, she never told me or anything, I guess she couldn't because if the other kids found out, they would be gossiping and all that, but I always thought she was gay and she was just great, she talked to me and she showed me that she understood. She would always say "just be who you want to be, don't worry about what other people think."

I had one lady who said "I think you are a beautiful person and don't let nobody tell you that you have to be with a man. If you want to be with whoever you want to be with, be what you want to be and don't let nobody stop you from being whatever."

Peers or Other Residents

Other adolescents living in the home, like professionals, were also identified by those in the study group as having negative and positive responses to their presence as gays/lesbians. It was clear that positive responses from peers were explicit when staff set a tone of acceptance, as Tina so aptly describes it:

I think that young people, adolescents, are more tolerant than adults and I think that they also actively look for adult cues. So the attitudes of adolescents will always actively reflect those of the adults who are supervising them. I think that when you put gay and lesbian adolescents together with heterosexually oriented adolescents there is always a normal checking-each-other-out kind of phase and always some conflict comes up whenever you get any adolescents together, but they can also look at the differences and talk about it as long as they have those cues that it is an okay thing to do.

The transmission of affirmative "cues" by staff members was corroborated by the professional staff interviewed, as the following suggests:

> Like many issues, kids do pick up a lot of cues from staff, so I think staff is important and I think if they pick up that what you're supposed to do is to put this kid down and deride them because they are different, then I think that's what they'll do.

> My experience with kids in group homes has been that they tend to be so accepting of differences that it's unbelievable. I find that when they start to have some negative reactions, a lot of times it's because of the adults around them and some of those feelings from around the adults. I think adults can project their negative feelings on to kids. Most kids are accepting, it's the staff that gets stuck on seeing that everything is sexual.

> If staff are okay, then the kids are okay. I think a lot depends, a big part depends on how the staff deals with the lesbian kids. If the staff are okay that this is really just another resident, then the kids are fine too. Most kids don't care if another kid is out. I don't feel that there is too much prejudice in the kids. It's more in the way staff act.

In out-of-home-care settings where there more than one resident was gay or lesbian, there was a sense that there was strength in numbers. Several young people commented on the importance of having more than one openly gay or lesbian in a group or foster home. The following excerpts illustrate the young people's thinking about this issue:

> Well, some would call me "faggot" and all or "you homo." They treat you different cause you're not like them, they are straight and you're gay so they wouldn't understand where you come from. Other gay kids know where I'm coming from. When I knew that there were other gay kids here I felt that I wasn't the only one than was going to be gay in the group home and it makes me feel better.

> There is one other gay resident where I live now, when I lived in Horizon House there were three of us. When you're not the only one it makes you feel more comfortable. Some of the more macho guys at first have a problem, but then they see that you're one of the guys just like they are, and they don't get all uptight.

> There are about four or five other gay kids in my group home, we had our ups and downs, it was the same. Being gay doesn't change the problems in

the world, everybody wants to be top dog and there is only room for one boss, you know? But when it comes time for us to stick together, we do. We had a little group that met and we used to discuss our problems and come together once a week that was good.

Study participants also observed that having other people like themselves made the environment a better fit:

The good thing about The Meadows is that some of them would tell me it's ok to be gay and that you don't have to feel bad because there are other people like you here.

Mixed Experiences

Staff

For some youngsters, their overall experience cannot be characterized as either positive or negative. Analogous to the response from most of society, these young people experienced a mixture of responses from staff, from peers, and from within the out-of-home-care environment. Staff responses to sexual orientation are varied:

The staff . . .Oh, God! Some of them was fair and some of them did their jobs, others didn't, some were just there for the paycheck. None of them talked to me about being gay. The female staff was better than the male staff. The female staff could see you as someone they could relate to or bug out with. With the male staff you can just forget it, they just don't want to be bothered period because you are gay, they just don't want to be bothered with you. They would never say things directly to me, but they would say little nasty things like—"that new fag kid that just came in, why do they make us put up with these gay children, why do they ship them here, no wonder their parents get rid of them." The other boys said things too, but I mean, we are at an age when we say those things to each other, but when other adults say those things to you, then that's something to think about, 'cause kids will say anything to get you upset, but when adults say it, it's different.

I had staff there that were gay and they supported me one hundred percent and there were other staff who didn't support me—they made me go in the bathroom by myself—they made me feel different, they made me feel like I was a freak or something, like I was a pervert. They didn't know about gay people, if they did they wouldn't have acted the way they do. They were ignorant. The only people I could talk to there were the other people who were gay; they supported me one hundred percent and told me what to expect from people and all.

With detectable pain, Tracey reflected on the mixed response he encountered from staff when he recalled his coming out experience:

Between the ages of fifteen and eighteen there was a whole lot of denial going on. I thought, not me, it couldn't be me, but it was. I started going with this male and it dawned on me that there was only one reason I was with this male, and there was no use denying it any longer. It made me come out to a staff member who I knew cared about me. He noticed a couple of things, like for one I spend the night at a friend's house and I came back with a neck full of hickeys, he's not stupid now, he asked me "How was the weekend?" And the first thing I said was "Nothing happened!" And he knew and he told me he knew, but I denied it. But then I got so tired of denying it and I said "I don't care what people think any more—this is me!" And I came out. Everyone was sort of surprised, or as we would say—they gagged, they were very surprised, mouths wide open. But what I didn't realize was that once they found out only one or two staff members gave me the same respect and liked me just the same, the others just treated me like an invisible kid. They were actually very cruel, cruel in the sense that I just become that invisible boy again, just like I was in my family.

Peers or Other Residents

Young gays and lesbians also had mixed experiences with their peers. One commented:

Straight kids tended to act like society, some were accepting, and some of them weren't.

Young gays and lesbians also indicated that their perceived initial responses from peers indicated some fear, as the following excerpts suggest:

At first they were afraid because I was gay, but once they got to know you and hang out with you, it's all right. Some of the guys were troublemakers and you just learned to stay away from them. There were other gay kids there also, at first I was the only one, and then after a couple of months they started to come in. When I first came, they had to get to know me and then they would say "Oh, he's cool." When the others started to arrive, they would ask me "Is he cool, can we be friends with him?" They would come up to me and ask me because I am gay, I should know everything about them, I'd say: "I don't know, why don't you talk to him and find out?"

I used to go into the group homes and never said it right away because I was afraid that I'd fucking have to deal with this again, right, all these fucking heterosexual people [laughs] that I would have to explain myself to. And the kids were like curious because I was their first official one they ever had.

Several professional respondents corroborated these perceptions. One social worker in New York commented:

Either they are very, very uptight about it or they are okay about it, comfortable with it. If they are comfortable with it, then they can talk about the issue and they will tell them that they have some friends who are gay, etc. The kids that are the most uncomfortable will us the terms . . . that are usually derogatory, I find these kids are most uncomfortable with their own sexuality.

Another professional in Los Angeles noted the range of responses that he observed occurring with respect to gay and lesbian adolescents in an out-of-home care setting:

I've seen two things happen, it goes from absolute ostracism which eventually comes to be absolute acceptance, like he or she is no big deal. The other scenario is that initially no one knows that the young person is gay or lesbian and they get to know them, and then they find out that they are gay. By that time they already know the person and it's no big deal.

Negative Experiences

By and large, the majority of young people interviewed expressed overall dissatisfaction with their out-of-home-care experience. Difficulties began immediately, at intake.

Intake and Lack of Welcome

Adolescents being admitted to a child welfare program are frequently fraught with anxiety and fear as they enter their new living situation. One of the most basic principles of group care for children asserts the importance of making newcomers feel welcome. Those who are openly gay and lesbian are often made to feel unwelcome, as Tracey recalled:

> I mean we don't exactly get the "Welcome Wagon" when we come to a group home. Gay and lesbian people are looked down upon. When a lot of people just look at us like that we have another strike against us.

Professional respondents corroborated this perception of the "welcome" into care experienced by gay/lesbian adolescents:

> In some cases, CWA has told us before the kid arrives that he is gay and then we tell the group home staff. We tell them to make sure that this child is welcomed. We also remind them that this is confidential and not to be shared with the residents, but when the kid arrives, all the kids already know. It's the staff, they start saying "Wait until you meet our new resident, wait till you see who's coming." Then, there's the big welcome, my guess is that they are brought into the child care office by the worker who is on duty and told "We've heard a little bit about your behavior and we don't allow that kind of behavior and if you try it, you'll get hurt, and if you try it, I can't guarantee your safety here." That's a hell of a welcome, wouldn't you say?

Young people who were open about their orientation reported that they were frequently greeted by staff as if they were aberrant and were admonished that they would be closely monitored. Maura, from New York, recalled her "welcoming" experience graphically:

> When I arrived at St. Mary's the people there really freaked out and accused me of being a rapist and some other shit and the people at Children's Haven didn't like it either. I mean in one placement, as soon as I walked in the door, I mean I wasn't even shown to my room, I was brought into the staff office and told by staff "You know we don't go for any of that mess around here—so you better watch yourself and don't be bringing none of that lesbian shit around here." In this other place, I mean every time I walked by the staff office I was told, "Keep your business to yourself," every time I walked by.

Katrina had a very similar experience:

> There was a group home called Trainor Street for women, and when I went
> there they outright told me it was an all female group home, and they just
> said, "Look, if there's any lesbian activity here you're out." I was like okay,
> but to tell you the truth, at that time all I wanted was stable housing, I did-
> n't give a fuck about my sexuality. Later I realized though how messed up
> it had been for them to say that.

Some young people reported being open about their sexual orientation at
intake, but when placed in the group home and confronted by peers and
staff, denied their identity. Tony recalled:

> Yeah, when they interviewed me they asked me if I was gay and I said yes,
> I am. They told me that was all right, I couldn't tell that it wasn't when they
> warned me about having sex with the other residents. They really seemed
> to be preoccupied with that. When I went to the group home and they
> asked me if I was gay I said, no. I told them I had a girlfriend. I just wasn't
> sure if they could deal with it or not, so I lied.

Some young people, like Kevin, reported that they were perceived by staff
to be gay or lesbian and pressured to disclose.

> Like if I was to tell a foster parent, it's like, they just don't, they don't know
> how to handle it. I was in this one foster home and I told them because they
> would always press me, "How come you don't have a girlfriend?" I'd say
> "Well I don't know I just can't find one at the time." Whenever they saw
> my friends at school who were, like, pretty feminine, my foster father
> would always ask: "Are they gay or something?" I would always say I did-
> n't know. But that was when I first moved there so I was, like, I'm not telling
> you nothing. But eventually I did.

Several young people reported that they were not welcomed into the
group home culture because they were too open. Janet, a young woman
from Toronto, equated her openness with nonacceptance:

> The reason I wasn't accepted in the agency was because I was very open
> about my sexuality and they were homophobic. I was not going to hide
> anymore and they just couldn't deal with me. After a while I got the mes-
> sage, I mean when it's obvious that you're not welcome, you eventual-
> ly leave.

The Need to Hide

Although each of the young people interviewed self-identified as gay or lesbian at the time of the interview, not all of them were straightforward about their orientation within the out-of-home-care systems wherein they lived. Similarly, whereas some of them had been certain from their initial placement onward about their sexual orientation, others were not as sure. During these interviews, it became clear that there were two sets of gays and lesbians in out-of-home care: those who were open about their sexual orientation and lived as openly gay or lesbian persons all the time; and those who were definite about their orientation, but felt vulnerable about disclosing their identity because they feared differential treatment from staff and peers. The thinking of the second group was expressed in remarks like: "You have to hide, to act straight. I went in there and I had to be Mr. Straight." Those who were open about their identity reported having a distinctly different experience from those camouflaged as heterosexual.

On the basis of their experiences, it was no wonder that the majority of these young people were determined at intake to conceal their sexual identity, as this passage suggests: "I think there's lots of gay and lesbian kids in care, but they hide, they hide for the same reasons I did. They may not be out but they are there."

The need to hide (also discussed in chapter 1) is deemed necessary for survival: first, because many fear staff and peer attitudes; and second, because they fear mistreatment, including verbal harassment and violence from both staff and peers. In fact, most of them reported that at one time or another they hid their orientation. The following excerpts from young persons in all three cities illustrate these points:

In Los Angeles:

> I had to hide, they knew, but they wouldn't accept it. They were totally against gays in that group home; they told me I was not allowed to talk about being a lesbian. They told me not to talk the way I do. They'd say to act like a so-called man. You can't come out and say what you are. Like you have to hide it. Even though I was out everywhere else I wanted to hide because there were staff and residents who made it difficult.

In Toronto:

> Yeah, I had to act totally straight 'cause a lot of the guys in there late at

night would go around a place like Church and Wellesley and they would like fag bash and all that and then come back and talk about it.

In New York:

> Everyone has this big wall up, especially when you're in a group home because you've lost a lot, you just don't want to get attacked so you don't come out, you've always got this barrier around you.

Peers, as Don's comments suggest, are sometimes unsure about their own sexual identity and are threatened by same-gendered sexuality:

> A lot of the guys in the group homes, they, they're either homophobic or they're like, like hiding it, they could be gay or like bisexual but they haven't come to terms with it themselves. I think about half of the kids in these group homes are gay. A lot of them are never going to tell you. They don't want this person to know that they are because they are afraid of how they will think about them.

Using a cover to hide your stigma, suggests Albert, is an effective technique of information control for those who are members of stigmatized groups:

> I was acting as straight as I could get and I never got bothered when I was at Kneter Home but when I was at Meyer House because I met this guy who I lived with for a while, he just blew my cover away . . . you have to hide, to act straight.

Keeping a careful watch to conceal evidence (Goffman 1963:94) that might blow your cover caused these young people to be extra careful about managing what they shared about themselves:

> You have to hide a lot of things. You have to hide a lot of papers and stuff, your personal stuff. I mean I could never have a button or anything that said gay or lesbian on it. A couple of times I wanted to pick up a copy of the *Pink Pages* and I didn't want to like take it back to the group home because it would be a dead giveaway.

> This one time, some of the kids set up one of the guys, they just thought he was gay. They went out and bought some books, threw them underneath his bed. The next day they went up and all said "Look what's under that

person's bed." And everyone goes "Yeah we knew he was a fucking fruit."
I wasn't sure if this guy was gay or not, but I knew that I was, and all I
thought was "Oh, God, that could have been me." I went and wrote a little note to staff, I just said that, "I'm not going to say who, but someone
from room 5 brought these books to set this person up." But my hand-
writing is terrible and people figured out that it was me who wrote the note.
So at that point, I had to come out.

Being able to hide one's stigma (Goffman 1963:87) has one benefit: it en-
ables those who are stigmatized, as the excerpts below suggest, to see and
to hear what the larger society says about them:

> I tried to hide it 'cause you'd be sitting around like watching a movie and
> these people are supposed to be like, I guess they want to call themselves
> role models or whatever, they are supposed to like I dunno, be model citi-
> zens. But you'd be watching a movie and there would be a gay scene on
> TV or something and they would start laughing and making fun of it and
> stuff like that and the other kids did also, so I'd try to laugh along, I just
> got fed up eventually. This happened in most of the places that I was in.
> I'd get fed up of seeing these guys laugh about it so finally I would say
> something and then after that I was kind of singled out all the time. They
> never really said things to mock me or anything but I noticed that the other
> kids would get treated better than I was and stuff like this. It wasn't like
> they came straight out and saying something it was their use of their au-
> thority to get at me.

> If you were gay, you got kicked out of the other ones—I mean you got ter-
> minated and kicked out. In one home a kid called me a fag, I got into a fight
> and the staff thought I might have been and they warned me that they
> would have to terminate me if I was. It made me closeted even more. I clos-
> eted myself well enough so they didn't know but they made homophobic
> comments and stuff: "Stupid faggots," "He is so gay." It made me think it
> was totally wrong; it scared me and put me back further—after all that who
> would want to come out?

Seeing firsthand how others viewed gays and lesbians causes many to conceal their identity even more. Fearing the reprisals of discrimination and violence provided Alejandro and Gayle with a major motivation for hiding:

> They have a lot of gay residents in these group homes, a lot of them try to
> hide, but I am able to tell who they are. I have seen a lot of gay kids in there,

they are just scared that the staff or the residents in there will act differently if they know. [April 1993]

I knew people in my foster home, and in my group home, who were gay but
they went out to make it look like they were not gay. They were hiding it.
They were afraid of getting beat up or discriminated against.

Staff Hostility

Those interviewed felt that, in most agencies, their sexual orientation was
not considered a proper topic for open discussion. Comments from Sharice
and Fred are representative:

I wasn't allowed to talk about homosexuality at all. They never let me address it in group meetings. I was told don't talk about it, it's not an issue,
it's not to be discussed here, but it was a big part of my life. It was all discussed behind closed doors. These were people that I had spent two years
with and I was not allowed to bring it up. At one point in a house meeting
all of the other kids started saying "So she's gay, why can't we talk about
that? What's the big deal," but it was the staff, they couldn't deal with it.
The staff didn't want to fucking deal with it at all.

In one group home, I was told that I would go to hell and that what I was
doing was wrong. The staff let me know that I was NOT supposed to talk
to them about being gay. I don't think they knew much anyway, but I was
told, in more ways than one, not to discuss this area of my life.

Not being able to talk about one's personal life was damaging to one's
self-esteem, as Wilma says:

They never wanted me to talk about it. If I talked about my girlfriends
they'd say I don't want to talk about that shit and I'd put my head down
and walk away.

In cases, when homosexuality was discussed, as evidenced by Robbie's
comment, they were told by staff that being gay was wrong:

They never talked to me openly about it, they said, "It's not right," that I
"shouldn't do it," but they say "You're good looking and all, you can have
anybody you want to." They were always putting gay people down, saying that they were sick and all, it was hard enough to have heard that from

my family, but now I had to deal with that in the group home too, it was too much.

Some of the messages sent to young people, like Shawn, were subtle, and some were more obvious:

No one ever came right out and talked to me about being gay, maybe a couple, well, in one place upstate, one lady upstate told me that being gay was wrong and that you shouldn't be gay and . . . other than that no one talked to me about it.

Overall, young people reported that it was stressful to be told that you're not supposed to talk about what's important to you; Raymond pointed out:

If I ever tried to talk about my boyfriend or what I did when I went out, I was told by staff "Don't be bringing that faggot shit out around here, you know we don't go for that." I couldn't even talk about what was important in my life.

Not being allowed to openly discuss their lives caused young people like Kevin to feel isolated:

There are so many gay people who feel left out because they feel that the counselors don't like them because they are gay and they felt like they are not loved and I hear a lot of people tell me that, they need a lot of help. I am gay and sometimes I don't feel loved, I sometimes feel that the straight people get more love than we do, I felt that in the group home, I felt that I was sometimes used by people.

Staff's Lack of Knowledge

Most child welfare professionals have an inadequate knowledge base about homosexuality. Staff's general misinformation and lack of viable information impedes them from providing adequate child welfare services to gay and lesbian youngsters as these excerpts suggest:

Staff do not have adequate or accurate knowledge of gay or lesbian people. I mean maybe they have worked with some gay people in the past, but I mean I would never feel comfortable opening up and saying that I met this guy or whatever.

I think one problem with these places is that they're run by psychiatrists. I went to see Dr. Parker and Dr. Hellman. They were at Central Hospital. Within fifteen minutes that I met Dr. Parker I walked out and told him to go fuck himself. He was telling me how sick and how disturbed I was because I am a lesbian and I must have been this and I must have been that and it had nothing to do with it. In the group home itself, they were always asking me: "Are you sure, are you sure you you're a lesbian, are you sure?" And I was like, "Yeah, I know." I went there when I was seventeen, I mean, I knew. They'd always come up to me and say "That's inappropriate" and "Are you really gay? I don't think you're gay. Are you seriously gay?"

Once they even sent me to this doctor who asked me questions about my sexuality, asked if I wanted a sex change, if I wanted to be a man, if I had a longing desire to have testicles and a penis and blah, blah, blah, blah. Then there are the staff that ask you all this personal stuff and it's really just for their own personal reasons. When I finally connected with one staff member, they would no longer allow me to work with her because they thought I was attracted to her. The whole experience was a nightmare.

I don't think they always understand, they say things like: "Why do you want to be gay? Why do you want to sleep with another man? What makes you so happy to be with another man?" And you tell them that is the way you was born and they say "That's bullshit, you can't be born gay." And I say "Yes you can!" And they say "How can you be born gay" and there's no way for me to prove it to them, so sometimes that can be difficult.

If all a gay kid knows about gay people is what he hears from straight people, then he's probably never going to figure out what he is. He will probably only know about the myths of homosexuality.

They were ignorant to me and to who I was about and it affected me. When I think back about those days, I get so mad because it hurts that no one paid attention to me being gay and it was a big part of my life.

Stereotypes and Myths Held by Staff

Lacking accurate information and a well-developed base of knowledge about homosexuality, many staff members believed the standard misinformation, including the usual myths and stereotypes, that was used to describe gay and lesbian orientation. For example:

I think that more staff members should learn a bit more about homosexuality, they should be a bit more open to it 'cause it's not like it's just a matter of who you had sex with, it's sort of a lifestyle and they need to realize that. It's not so much that people don't like homosexuals, but a lot of people have the wrong perceptions . . . like they think that all homosexuals are going to try to turn them out . . . like all they want to do is have sex with you or they snap their fingers and say "Miss Thing" or they think . . . I mean they have the wrong perceptions.

All of these staff just look for the fem boy or the butch girl. I think that's all they know about gay and lesbian people is what they see on TV. They have no information at all.

Some heterosexual professionals, even those who were perceived as sensitive by gay and lesbian young people, continued to look for stereotypical images. Don's comments are representative:

I mean even the director of the program where I live now, he's great and he's straight, but I don't think he can always tell if a kid is gay or not. They just can't tell who is gay and who isn't, unless they are really flamboyant and you know—stereotypical, loud, and wild.

Inequality of Treatment by Staff

Young gays and lesbians I interviewed said they wanted to be treated like everybody else. The majority, however, said they were treated differently once staff knew of their sexual orientation:

If a gay or lesbian kid lives in a group home, the staff has an attitude toward that person. They all should be treated the same because they are all human beings, but gay and lesbian kids are not treated that way.

Those interviewed told of numerous situations that served as reminders of how they differed. Trevor reported sensing a distancing from staff:

Yeah, for some reason, I mean I feel distance now. I mean I don't really hang around the house very much and people think I am being distant from them. They think that for the simple fact that I am not straight like they are, that I cannot hang out with them and that I can't understand.

In some cases they related this differential experience to being given funds for clothing shopping, as Julia and Mike reported:

A person that is not gay, you just sit back and watch and say why should she have more than me? Why should she go clothes shopping and get more than me? I feel that they should not knock somebody just because they are gay.

They treat you like, well, they don't care about you at all, they are prejudiced. Okay, for one, you know how in group homes you go shopping and stuff? Well, they spend more money on the straight kids than on the gay kids. They buy you cheap, cheap, clothes and the other kids, they buy them real expensive clothes and when it's time to go shopping they just keep putting you off, and off, and off. They let you wear filthy clothes and all. Attitude-wise they treat you differently.

Tamil introduced the concepts of "throwing shade" and "reading" someone who treats you differently:

They do treat you differently 'cause you are gay. They have a lot of activities like going to the gym and stuff, and if they feel it's too manly, then they are gonna throw some shade at you [give you attitude], but then you have to read them [tell them off] and then wait until we get to where we are going to show them that just because I am gay, I can play basketball, lift weights, they think because you are gay that you are not supposed to do all that.

Eddie's observations capture the perception that straight kids were treated one way, gay and lesbian kids another way:

I thought I was treated differently. I don't think that they are treated equally. I mean they made it so obvious. They just treated us differently. The straight kids were treated one way and the gay kids another way. I wish that there were gay and lesbian staff. They would have been more understanding.

Wilma felt that straight young people got staff's attention more quickly:

The girls that was gay were treated kinda differently, yeah, I did see a little change when they knew. Let's say that a gay girl was having a problem or something, or needed something and then a straight girl went to a counselor and said she needed this, they would give it to her faster than a gay girl. If you ask me, I don't know why is that, is it discrimination because of what a person want to be. I don't know, but that's just how it was, I did see that.

Fred recalled in vivid detail how some gays were jettisoned by the system:

Gay kids were treated there like they were treated in every other place, like they were foreign. They get respected by a few people, those people who are color blind, race blind, all of that, but there are very few of those people, a lot of people tend to do it just because of peer pressure you know, and that happens a lot in those kind of places because everybody's young you know. Gay kids get dumped on a lot I think if staff really knew gay kids, they would see that they are not afraid to get into things, I think they would categorize gay kids as generally being god. So they definitely spread more sunshine. But like I said, a lot of people are ignorant and don't know gay people, all they see is different and then they treat them differently.

Staff and Impact of Race, Culture, and Religion

Religion is a powerful force in society. In general, organized religions have condemned homosexuality and maintain that it is a morally unacceptable "lifestyle." Paula's recollection spoke to these sentiments:

> Staff in the group homes don't talk with the kids about being gay because they think it's wrong. A lot of people who work in these foster care agencies are Christian, you know—high, high Christians—Baptists and all, they don't believe in gay. They say it's a shame, it's against God and they don't want to talk about it.

Raul noted that the more "religious" a staff member was, the more unlikely it was for him or her to deal positively with those who were homosexually oriented:

> The only negative was this one guy, who was this religious guy, he was like a priest and like at first he was talking to me in conference about God and stuff and I told the director and he got in trouble because he wasn't supposed to do that. At times he would leave Bibles on my bed and readings about homosexuality and stuff, he got in trouble for that.

Richard defiantly made this declaration with respect to staff members and their religious beliefs:

> If they are so into God and God is love and all then they should make sure that they treat people better. They say that God don't make no mistake. It was no mistake to make me a gay black man.

Racial and cultural biases which were perceived as playing a role in the development of negative attitudes toward gays and lesbians were identified by adolescents from all races. Ralph, a Caucasian, made this comment:

I have been in about six different agencies. They treat you like, well, they are just there for the money, they don't care about the kids, so if you're white and gay or black gay, they don't care about you at all, they are all prejudice. They call you white trash, you white homo, they say you are garbage, call you all kinds of names.

Young people identified individuals from several Caribbean countries as particularly antigay and antilesbian, as Miguel's comments imply:

The Jamaicans, the West Indians, they is the worst! I mean they just hate gay and lesbian people. I don't know what it is about them, I guess it's just part of their culture. I know that this is true, because I have friends who are Jamaican and West Indian and they told me that people from their countries are real hard on homosexuals.

Katrina, an Aborigine Canadian, made this comment:

There were two-spirited people there, some did come out, but actually that was only the women. The boys, never, they never did. They wouldn't say anything about what they were because there was so much hatred in the Native group home, I think they wouldn't even have known.

While this data suggests that there are perceived connections between antihomosexual sentiment and various cultural groups, Annin (1990) cautions that individuals in the child welfare field must be careful about depicting homophobia as cultural (as contrasted with societal) in African-American/African-Canadian and Latino communities: to ascribe homophobia to African-American/African-Canadian and Latino men without including white men is racist. White men are also homophobic. While the cultures and races represented in this study undoubtedly have some negative feelings about homosexuality, they are not alone, as many cultures from Europe and Asia also espouse antihomosexual sentiment.

Impact of Staff Gender

According to those interviewed, male staff had a more difficult time accepting homosexuality than did female staff (Reiter 1991). Overwhelmingly, the comments of most young people concurred with Reiter's findings and suggested that female professionals were better suited to working with gays and lesbians than were male workers. Control issues and macho attitudes were identified as impairing male staff members' ability to care for young gays and lesbians. The following excerpts illustrate this point:

> The men staff they are prejudice, they are not capable of understanding I think. My social worker was pretty cool he works for me instead of against me, the house staff though brings me down. The house supervisor before he didn't know I was gay, he treated me different.

> I found in the group homes it was mostly the male staff that had a problem. I liked most of the female staff that worked there. A lot of them actually pulled me aside and talked to me about the male staff's attitudes and they told me not to mind the other staff and assured me that they would bring it up in a staff meeting and get it taken care of.

> I think the women staff are better in dealing with gay kids than the men. There are a lot of women staff in our house and they have raised gay kids before, so it's not new to them, so I guess they do have a little bit of knowledge.

> When the male staff got to bugging me about it, then the rest of the kids started too. I actually ran away from a couple of group homes because I didn't like it.

> There was a female staff member, I think she was actually a lesbian herself, I'm not sure. She held a big meeting about it because we were trying to talk about it and I was pissed off 'cause I was arguing with the kids just before that trying to stand up for my rights and stuff. I said that we should have a meeting about this but when we tried all the residents got crazy. They were all really close-minded about it. Then I got really upset and started screaming and things just got way out of hand and so she canceled the meeting.

Peer Responses

Acceptance by peers is very important to young people (Blos 1980; Germain 1991). The heightened importance of the peer culture during adolescence is an important factor in the increased motivation for conformity to the values, customs, and fads of the peer culture.

Heterosexual peers often act in a hostile manner toward gay and lesbian youth placed in their group home or foster home. Young men considered effeminate or young women considered masculine are frequently harassed by heterosexual peers. Unlike other adolescents who encounter difficulty with peers because of race, disability, personal appearance, and so on, lesbian and gay youth usually cannot turn to their families or staff for support. The following examples illustrate these points:

> With all of the criticism about faggot this and faggot that, the ones who are saying that are the ones who are usually doing it. But there is a lot of harassment also.

> In my group home there were a lot of arguments. The straight kids were always picking on the gay kids, calling them names, trying to set them up, constantly at them day in and day out. It was really unpleasant living there with them.

> The kids at The Mission were real bitches, I mean they were horrible, there were physical threats, mental threats, lots of verbal abuse. So I dashed out of there as soon as I could, I got my lawyer to get me out of there as soon as possible. At Talcott Center the kids never even got a chance to know me because I was immediately isolated from all of them.

Staff members corroborated these negative experiences by noting:

> I guess more the adolescent boys than the girls. A lot of these kind of tough guys, in my experience, have intimidated these guys in some way either verbally or physically. In some situations kids would just ignore the gay kid, some though are really hostile, ostracized him and make cracks about him. I always felt that those kids had a lot of homosexual fears within themselves and that a gay kid just triggered a lot of those feelings within them. Some of the staff kind of very silently supported some of the hostile feelings.

One staff respondent further noted that even being perceived as gay or lesbian led to many a young person's feelings of isolation:

> There have been cases where kids have been ostracized or victimized to some extent because they are accused of being gay or because they are involved with someone, that there is sexual activity made public, or maybe there are mannerisms that they see as being gay.

Environmental Factors That Cause a Good Fit

> This is a place where things are positive and where I can be myself.

Although this was not a comment that was resoundingly heard from each and all fifty-four interviewees, it would be equally inaccurate to report that every one of them experienced a poor fit within the out-of-home-care environment where he or she was placed. Although only 9% (n=5) reported having a positive experience throughout their sojourn in out-of-home-care placements, by the time these interviews were conducted, 52% (n=28) said that they had found a good fit because they had settled within environments that provided them with the support and sustenance necessary to thrive.

Certain young people found that there were implied cues and, in some cases, outward symbols that distinguished an environment as nurturing and safe. These were those who had experienced multiple placements, which involved moving from placement to placement until the environment that forged the right fit was found. Such environments were found in all three cities, but were limited to settings that were openly gay and lesbian affirming, or settings where there were openly gay or lesbian staff members. The majority of young people in these positive environments indicated that these were places where "you could be yourself," as evidenced by Tony:

> This is the best place to be if you have to be in a group home because you can be yourself. I felt like I was the only one in other group homes, no one heard what I was saying. Because everybody here is gay we all had problems and we all have to deal with it. We had staff even staff who weren't gay who wouldn't say things to hurt our feelings. We all understand each other here.

Others maintained that environments that permitted them to be themselves, and provided them with nurturance, facilitated their personal growth. Barb said:

> You can be more open and be your self. You don't have to hide, you can be yourself, accept yourself and be who you are. In other places, I could but some things I had to keep to myself. Here you can express yourself more and people know what you've been through. You can learn from the role

models, they are openly gay, you don't have to guess what their sexual orientation is, you know.

Jared echoed these sentiments:

> I have been here for three weeks. I wasn't really open, but I knew I needed to be in a better environment. This is different from any other place—it's more supportive and it's a good environment.

The chorus that "it's okay to be gay" was proclaimed by several. Sharte indicated that it was at first hard to believe that it was true:

> Honey, when I first arrived they said it was okay to be gay here and I thought, oh sure. But I found out that it really was, I couldn't believe it. I have had my problems with staff about a lot of things, but never about being gay. They are fine in that regard, they might be bitches in other things, but in that are they are fine.

Steven reported that being gay in his current group home placement was not a sensationalized event:

> In the group home that I am in now, it's okay to be gay, so the staff and the other guys who are not gay are not at all uptight about gay people. I can talk to the staff there, because I know they care about me, they don't care if I'm gay or not, that's really not a big deal because like I said, being gay there is okay.

Tamil recounted feeling a sense of relief at finding such an environment:

> When I came here, they told me it was okay to be gay, but I didn't believe them. At first I thought that it was gonna be like all of the other places, so I tried to hide, but it wasn't necessary, it really was okay to be gay here. I felt great, I could be who I am for the first time and not worry about people finding out my secret.

Being able to let your guard down was seen by Alex as an indicator of an environment that promoted a good fit:

> When you're at Meyer House or something, you're always talking and just kind of, you always got that barrier because you're gay. You don't want anybody to know because you don't want anybody pointing their finger at you.

> When you're in a place that's all right for gay people, it's better because you're not hiding behind anything. There's no barriers. You don't have to . . . you can be open, honest.

The old adage "There's no place like home" seemed to ring true for several. Angelo described the quintessence of living within a nurturing out-of-home-care environment:

> Places like this help people to accept others as they are. It helps you build self-esteem and it even helps your parents to accept you. It's a home away from home.

In New York, Raymond agreed:

> I came into placement because I wasn't getting along with my mother . . . it wasn't like I got thrown out or anything, I mean I love my mother, but I just had to leave. I heard about this group home from my friend and I went there and I was accepted. At first I was scared because I had heard all of these things about group homes, but it was like one big family, it was, it was like one big family.

Environments That Do Not Constitute a Good Fit

Young gays and lesbians generally noted the lack of signs indicating that it was safe to be open about their sexual orientation. Just as they looked for cues from staff and peers, many also scanned their environments for signs of safety and acceptance. When they determined that it was not safe, they concealed their identity. In recalling their sense of poor fit within the out-of-home-care environment, many reflected on a plethora of negative environmental experiences. Joyce's experience provides a summary of the range of negative environmental elements:

> It was all very subtle really, well sometimes it was blatant, and sometimes it was subtle. First of all, whenever a straight kid wanted to talk about their girlfriend or their boyfriend it was fine, but when I wanted to talk about this girl I met, they all acted like they were totally disgusted by me. I mean, the message was clear—"We do not want to hear about your kind of sexuality." Second, there was never any recognition that gay or lesbian people existed. I mean I was out and they still tried to deny that I existed.

They never included information about gay or lesbian sexuality when they spoke about human sexuality, they never spoke about HIV/AIDS education that included discussions about gay or lesbian people—we were always just left out. Third, they never had any kind of gay or lesbian affirming posters or anything—I mean I'm not talking about having a poster of two guys kissing or anything, I just mean something which acknowledged that gay people existed. Whenever I suggested it, they all just put on this big face and said "No way!" I guess it wasn't a very accepting place.

Safety was clearly identified as a matter of concern for Tina:

There was no indication that it was a safe place. There was an assumption that I was heterosexual and there were no posters, nothing in the agency that would let me knows that it was safe for me to be open about being a lesbian. No, there were no posters—other things to make it feel safe. Definitely, the major thing that I found was that workers needed to use neutral language, say "are you dating?" It was assumed that I was dating a guy. It needs to be said it's ok for you to be gay, lesbian, or bisexual here. If they are, it is so important to do that. Posters are so important—even if you are afraid there's still a number to call.

As if ignoring one's existence was not painful enough, Carl reported that there were other environmental factors that constituted a poor fit that were more distressing.

I'd sit down on the couch and they'd sit beside me and then they'd realize who they were sitting beside and move. This one woman, I had a bitch of a time with. I worked so damn hard to get her to understand that I'm okay, I'm not going to give her the cooties or nothing, I'm not going to make a pass at her, she was very homophobic, she didn't know how to deal with it. I mean do you know what it is like to have to live in a place like that? Do you know how it feels? I mean I couldn't live at home with my own family because of who I am and then to get treated like that by people who are suppose to be professional and trained to deal with kids. I just don't think it's fair. It's just not right.

Geographic Factors

Corresponding with the concept of migration to a new environment as an adaptive strategy to facilitate a good fit (Germain 1981; Hartmann 1958), geographical location seemed to indicate a goodness of fit for some. Those interviewed noted that out-of-home-care settings located in urban areas seemed to be more accepting of gays and lesbians than suburban or rural areas. Young people from all three cities commented on the openness of urban environments.

In New York Eddie asserted:

> I mean the Village is the capital of the gay world. So, when I came here, I felt at home for the first time. I was so happy that my group home was close to the Village.

Similarly, Brenda (Los Angeles) said:

> L.A. is pretty cool. Even though we get carefully supervised here in this group home, the fact that we are near West Hollywood and the center of gay life in L.A. is important. I mean I came from a real red-neck part of California and there was no way that I could have ever came out there.

Although Celine and Philip, from the Toronto area, specifically noted the openness of their city:

> I came to Toronto because Toronto's very open-minded.

> Toronto is the gay capital of Canada so it's easy to be gay here.

Alex, another young gay from Toronto, disagreed:

> In this city? No, I would not be open, but in Montreal I would, that's where I learned to be more open.

One emerges from compiling these accounts of the experiences of gay and lesbian adolescents in out-of-home care with a sharpened sense of the diverse ways that they have found or not found "a sense of fit" in their lives. Our knowledge is enriched by these young people's examples. This group of gay and lesbian adolescents in out-of-home care expands our capacity to explicate and portray varied phenomenon that occur within institutional settings for young people. In doing so, they dispel a powerful myth that Canadian-U.S. child welfare systems propose—that child welfare systems *care for all children*. These narratives undermine other false-hoods as well, namely that gay and lesbian adolescents do not exist in child welfare settings and further, as these data show, that most young gays and lesbians are already in care and do not generally come into placement because they have been thrown out of their own homes.

A parallel inference that surfaces in exploring these experiences is that heterocentism—the privilege of heterosexual relations over gay or lesbian identities—continues to stigmatize and malign these young people because they have refused or have been unable to "fit in" to systems that were designed to meet the needs of heterosexual young people. Although a minority of those I interviewed had positive, or at best mixed, experiences in out-of-home care, the bulk of the group reported experiences marked by personal denigration from both staff and peers, as well as institutional intolerance and prejudice. Most of them lived under suspicion of arrested development or perversion, compelled to justify their identity, to explain their sexual orientation, to prove their femininity or masculinity, and in general to defend their normality.

The search for a good fit, to conform, is draining and consumes a great deal of energy. This search has not, however, succeeded in subjugating these young gays and lesbians. Instead, they have configured their lives in their own terms, against all odds. They have had to endure name-calling, verbal and physical abuse, subtle and blatant discrimination. Those who continually found a poor fit within out-of-home-care settings continued their search for affirming environments. In many cases, as we shall see, these young people fled to the streets to recreate their own versions of "family."

CHAPTER 4

|Escaping a Poor Fit: Harassment and Violence|

Constantly negotiating life in an environment where the threat of violence is an ever-present reality, the gays and lesbians I interviewed said they never felt completely secure or confident. Their sense of safety in out-of-home-care settings is tenuous and fragile. Violence is used to inflict punishment and enforce compliance or conformity to the norms of the family or the child welfare system. For many, verbal harassment causes as much hurt as physical violence because it profoundly damages self-esteem.

Many young people enter foster care because it offers sanctuary from abusive family relationships and violence that occurs in their homes. Rindfleisch (1993:265) writes: "Once in placement, children and youths are presumed to be in an environment superior to that from which they were removed. So they are not thought to need protection beyond that provided by state licensing activities." For too many youngsters, the brutality they experienced prior to coming into care did not stop once they enter the system.

Young lesbians and gays, unlike their heterosexual counterparts, are targeted for attack specifically because of their sexual orientation (Comstock 1991; Garnets et al. 1992; Herek and Berrill 1992). U.S. and Canadian culture, pervaded by a heterocentric ideological system that denies, denigrates, and stigmatizes gays and lesbians, simultaneously makes them invisible and legitimizes hostility, discrimination, and even violence against them. Safety has always been an issue for gays and lesbians. They must assess issues of safety in their lives on an everyday basis. When they indulge in behaviors acceptable for heterosexuals (such as walking down a street holding hands or kissing), they make public what Western society has prescribed as private. They are accused of flaunting their sexuality and are thereby perceived as deserving of or even asking for retribution, harassment, or assault.

The fifty-four participants in my study reported that verbal harassment was often inaugurated at home within their own family systems. Many said that relatives and sometimes even acquaintances in their community helped to increase the momentum of this violence by joining in the harassment. The extent to which they experienced verbal harassment and physical violence in foster care placements, by their peers in and in some cases by the very staff responsible for caring for them, is astounding. The stigma attached to being gay or lesbian often prevented them from reporting their victimization. Many said that when the abuse was reported, it was the victims themselves who were blamed. Consequently, more than half of the young people in this study chose, at some point in time, the apparent safety of the streets.

Tirades from family members, peers, and some staff members that began with the taunts ("you fucking faggot," "bulldyke," "homo," and "queer") in some cases escalated into punches, burnings, and rape. Gays and lesbians who were deemed "disposable individuals," deserving of being "jostled into line" or "kept in the closet," frequently found environments so poor and the fit so bad that many felt as though they literally had to flee for their lives. Some of those who looked for a safer environment found the safety and fit they wanted; others found an "even less favorable complementarity" (Meyer 1996).

Fear for Personal Safety

Is it safe for gays/lesbians living in group homes or congregate care settings to self-identify as gay/lesbian? Of those interviewed, 78% of the adolescents and 88% of the child welfare professionals said that it was not safe. One professional (New York) linked the issue of safety with the phenomenon of hiding:

> In most agencies, it's just not safe for a gay or lesbian young person to be identified. If the other kids know that they are gay or lesbian . . . they harass them, or worse. Sometimes when the staff find out they either treat the young person differently or close their eyes to some of the situations which occur after-hours. It's just not safe for them to be out and because they are not out, then the staff believe that they don't exist.

Another practitioner (California), concurred and associated fear with issues of safety for the young people when she made this comment:

I think that they feel alienated, and that they fear for their lives. I think that they feel that there is no one on staff that they can turn to and that they are even tentative about talking to their social worker for fear that it will be told to the administration. I think that it is interesting to note that no one in this agency has ever come out to the medical department or the mental health department personnel. Most kids here would come out to their social worker if they came out to anyone. Most gay kids quickly access that there is really no one to tell.

Young people in all three cities agreed that they felt a sense of real fear in gays and lesbians. Several noted that although some of their peers were open about their sexual orientation in social settings away from their group homes, they were closeted in their out-of-home setting. Steven commented:

People are afraid to tell people that they are gay. I mean I used to hang out in the Village with boys from my group home, but we never talked about being gay. The staff didn't know that we were gay. You made sure some of them didn't know because then they would make your life miserable. I tell you, sometimes the staff people were worse than the kids were.

Geoffery, from Toronto, made an almost identical remark:

There were these guys in my group home that were always giving me a hard time and then I'd see them hanging out on Wellesley. They'd say, "Hey don't tell anybody, all right?" They were out downtown, but not out in the group home. I didn't mind keeping their secret, but I always let them know that they needed to stop the shit that they were pulling in the house. Usually I had no problems with them after that. The staff people were so hard on gay kids.

In Los Angeles, Angelo made similar comments about the dual nature of his peers both inside and outside the group home environment with respect to their fears:

I knew people in my foster home and group home who were gay but they went out of their way to make it look like they were not gay. They were hiding it. They were afraid of getting beat up or discriminated against. There was a guy in my group home—he had a girl but we dated secretively. Being in a group home or a foster home is hard because if you can't tell the staff or a parent or brother who you are gay because they might beat upon you or discriminate against you.

Rejection at Intake

Professional staff I interviewed noted that gay or lesbian adolescents are frequently denied admission into a program, or they are "got rid of" once their homosexual orientation is discovered. Not surprisingly, 89% (n=48) of the young people interviewed indicated that they were re-placed or they themselves awoled from their initial placement because they were treated unfavorably, either by staff or peers, because of their sexual orientation.

Although both New York City and Los Angeles have antidiscriminatory laws prohibiting discrimination based on sexual orientation, several professionals said that their agencies did not admit self-identified gay or lesbian youngsters. They indicated that the reason their agencies denied admission to a gay or lesbian was a safety issue. Comments such as the following are typical of the bias against young gays/lesbians:

> We have not accepted any openly gay or lesbian youngsters. I think our policy has been that we have decided not to accept openly gay youngsters . . . the response that we have gotten from the other kids was so negative that it was hard to assure them that they were safe . . . so we decided not to take those who made an outright declaration.

Child welfare professionals have historically used the rationalization that they cannot protect a gay kid from the other kids as a reason for not welcoming an openly gay/lesbian into their program. One administrator in a New York child welfare agency said:

> The agency in the past had a policy that if a child was overtly homosexual or lesbian that they would not take them into the agency. And the reason was that we could not guarantee their safety. It wasn't that their behavior was a problem, it's a safety issue because the other kids would gang up on them, the other kids would beat up this kid. They were concerned about that from a realistic management point of view.

Once again, the theme of gay and lesbian young people not being "welcomed" was noted. With respect to using the issue of safety as an exclusionary device, professionals rarely noted that it was the behavior of the perpetrators and not the gay or lesbian that staff needed to address. A Los Angeles professional explained it this way:

> Gay and lesbian kids didn't feel welcomed, and were seen as troublemakers, in fact I had a kid for two days in one place, and I had a worker call me

up and say "I can't have this kid here because the other kids want to beat him up." I said: "Has this person done anything inappropriate?" And they said "no." And I said: "It sounds like your other kids are planning to do something inappropriate and are expressing it, maybe that's what you should be addressing." So the kid . . . he comes into the agency and is immediately seen as the disruptive force. That has been the major problem all these years is that the agencies are so afraid that this one kid . . . or "I can't have this boy here because the other kids will want to beat him up because they don't like faggots."

Verbal Harassment

Within the Home

As discussed in chapter 1, many gays and lesbians perceive that they are different even as young children. This difference separates them from their own families. In response to their perceived difference, families, who prescribe conformity amongst members, frequently engage in verbal harassment as a means to keep them in line (Savin-Williams 1994). Gayle, a 19-year-old from New York, was warned to remain closeted:

> I told my grandmother that I was gonna come out of the closet and she said, "Girl, you better get right back in!"

Young people recalled with vivid and often painful exactness the experience of verbal antilocutions made against them by their immediate family members. Sharte remembered his mother's bitterness toward his behavior, which he had considered as normal:

> I was eight when I entered foster care. It was the relationship between me and my mother that was the primary reason for me coming into fostering care. We never talked about me being gay or anything, but there were certain things that my mother would say to me, that let me knew, she knew. She would say things like "Stop being a little girl," you know. Things like, "You little sissy, I'm not raising a little girl, I'm not raising no punk."

The experience seemed to be standard for young women as well as for young men. Maura told a comparable story of parental rejection:

> My mother couldn't deal with the fact that I was a dyke, that's why I came into placement. She kept saying, "Why can't you act like a girl?" I mean,

she was always trying to get me to wear dresses and stuff, I mean, I just didn't feel comfortable. Every time I wore a dress I felt like a guy in drag. I just wished she could have let me be myself.

The metaphor of the "throw-away child" was common within the narratives of several young people who used "garbage metaphors" to describe their treatment by their families. Recalling the experience of feeling "dumped on," Tracey said:

> My relationship with my family was not the greatest. I guess the best way to describe my relationship with my family was, they were the dump truck and I was where they dumped all of their garbage. No one ever paid any attention to me unless they were mad, and then they would scream at me and dump on me. It wasn't that great. They had suspicions that I was gay, they told me I had effeminate ways, which I don't really think are effeminate, I'm sensitive and I have a very big heart and a lot of people look at that as effeminate.

Raul, a Puerto Rican, recalled the verbal abusiveness of his mother when he came out to her:

> I have known that I am gay all of my life, but when I came out to my mother, she was not able to accept that fact, she went wild, screaming *maricon*, *pendejo*, all of these really terrible curses, I was her only son and all. She threw all of my clothes out in a big plastic garbage bag and threw me out. I had nowhere to live.

The metaphor of disposal youth became a reality in Tamil's case:

> My grandmother started to tell me to stop acting like a fucking faggot. I didn't think I was doing anything wrong, I mean I wasn't even going out with guys at the time. She was always harping on me telling me to act like a boy and to stop acting like a little girl, and one day she just said, "I am sick of putting up with your faggot-ass ways and I want you out of my house," she had all of my clothes thrown in those black plastic garbage bags and all sitting by the door.

Although the majority of gay and lesbian young people I interviewed did not enter placement because they had been thrown out of their homes, the threat that their disclosure might prompt such a reaction from their families was always a fear that kept many "in line" and in the closet.

Foster and Adoptive Parents

Foster parents and even adoptive parents were not above engaging in verbal harassment. A New York child welfare professional recalled the harassment she had witnessed on her caseload:

> In one home, I remember that a boy placed there was unmercifully harassed by his foster mother. She kept picking on him about dating girls, about the way he held his hands, about the way he spoke, she kept telling him that "you don't want people to think you are that way, right?" She was relentless. The harassment escalated to the point that the youngster finally asked to be removed from the family. The foster mother just could not be persuaded that what she was doing was harmful to him—she thought she was guiding him.

Another practitioner, also from New York, acknowledged that some foster parents asked to have young people removed from their homes if they perceived them to be gay or lesbian:

> I'm sure that there are a lot of kids who are thrown out of foster homes because the foster parent feels they are gay. On occasion we have had foster parents say that when they found them in the room with another male, they were just scared to death and immediately asked to have that child removed and the child was tossed from foster home to foster home.

Remee, from Los Angeles, told of her own real life experience:

> There was only one foster home that I was in that it was bad. They found out I was gay 'cause I was talking on the phone to my girlfriend. The foster mother heard our conversation and immediately told my roommate to move out of our room. She said she thought I might get into a mood and want to have sex with her. I mean we had been roommates for two years. I wasn't attracted to her. But to make matters worse, then she called the agency to ask to have me removed because she said she didn't have a license to have gay people in her home.

Out-of-Home-Care Settings

Verbal harassment was so commonplace in group homes, foster homes, and congregate care settings that most young people almost forgot to mention it. All but one said that they had been the victims of verbal harassment because of their sexual orientation. Recalling the experience of verbal harassment with peers in his group home, Wilem said:

> We had to go through a lot with them. The name-calling was just a given. I almost didn't even think to mention that because it always happened. I had fights several times, but the verbal harassment it is regular.

Barb, from Los Angeles, said that the verbal harassment she experienced in her group home placement came from both peers and staff:

> They'd call me dyke, nasty pussy, the staff and the kids. The kids would say if you look at me I'll fuck you up. The staff would do nothing—they'd say, "That's what you get for being gay."

Don made the distinction between being verbally or physically assaulted with this comment:

> I was verbally bashed, not physically. People calling me faggot and all that. I remember feeling really pissed off when this one counselor always called me a faggot.

Peers or Other Residents

Being different from your peers is hard when you are an adolescent because adolescents seldom tolerate difference. Overwhelmingly (93%), the gay and lesbian adolescents interviewed experienced a great deal of verbal harassment from other residents. The comments of one young man from New York are representative of many:

> You know they was always fuckin' with you making my life miserable. You know, they called me faggot and homo and saying things like get the fuck away from me, don't look at me, stuff like that.

Many young people reported that the harassment was so common that they got used to it. Patrick recalled:

> I always got teased by the other guys, you know, the usuals, faggot, queer, homo, I hate to say it, but eventually you got used to it.

James, an African American from New York, thought of his ability to adapt to constant verbal abuse by describing it as a "protective shield":

Kids noticed that I was not like other kids, they thought I was weird, then out came all of those negative words: faggot, homosexual, you know, this and that. In every group home I have been in there has been harassment, but I learned to put up a shield and ignore it. But inside I remember it.

Gayle observed that verbal harassment was a more commonplace experience for males than for females:

I know a boy in school who is gay and the other boys really bother him and tease him, I feel sorry for him. But that doesn't happen to girls, because people can't tell with girls. I think that people are afraid of real butch girls, so they don't bother them.

Maura, however, had a different experience:

When I was upstate, every time I walked by this one cottage, they would be yelling out "dyke" or yelling "where's your motorcycle?" Then they would all start making motorcycle sounds and shit like that. I couldn't take it.

Child welfare staff members corroborated these accounts of other adolescents' verbal abusiveness:

That's why in this particular program that they don't admit being gay. Because this particular population would definitely be rough on them. When we bring it up, they laugh at the subject and make little cracks and things like that and you can tell the kids in the room who are kind of dealing with the subject, but they are so denigrated by the other kids that they would never come forth.

Another child welfare professional suggested that the jokes helped to erode a gay's or lesbian's sense of self-esteem:

There's jokes, sometimes there are intolerable jokes, both practical jokes and verbal jokes. It's really rough for gay kids. The other kids really torture them. It really gets to them. I have had kids who come back to their rooms after a weekend home visit and have antigay graffiti written on their walls, condoms filled with dishwashing liquid put on their doorknob, you know, just plain harassment.

The "Welcoming" Process

Most young people reported that the verbal harassment and antilocutions were worse when they first arrived at the group home. Wilem recalled:

> Up at Mount Laurel, there was a lot of verbal harassment, especially at first when I first came, then it dropped off, that was until they were angry with me, then it would all start up again: "You fuckin' homo," "Suck my dick," you know, stuff like that.

Alex also found that the name-calling was worse at first, but that it abated as peers got to know who he was:

> Well, at first you get the name-calling—homo, faggot—all that, but after I spoke to a lot of them and I found out that first of all a lot of them just don't understand or like they hear the myths and misconceptions that they think are true, and none of them, like knew me personally, and after I spoke to them they were like—Oh! Once they see where you are coming from they accept it, well, not maybe accept it, but, you know, they open up.

Some reported that their peers alluded to their fear of diseases as a factor in the process of verbal harassment. The myth that HIV illness and AIDS are "gay diseases" remains a powerful falsehood:

> Well, they were like, what they would call me is "faggot," or "you homo," or "you suck this or you suck that." The straight kids were always saying things like "Just keep your faggot shit on that side of the room, don't be bring none of your faggot diseases or faggot shit in here."

Jared's experience, which suggested that his peers used religion as a justification for their harassment, contains a comment that was frequently heard:

> I had to deal with a lot of verbal abuse—"you faggot"— or kids telling me, "You should be ashamed of yourself" or the religious fanatics saying, "You are an abomination against the Lord." The breaking point came when I started working, I mean, I was out all day working, and then I had to come back and listen to this shit—that's when I said forget it and I left.

Several of these gays and lesbians noted that some of their peers seemed deliberately to try and instigate trouble. Laurence remarked:

> Sometimes they would try to start trouble and say that you were looking at them when you're not even looking at them. I would say, "I'm not looking at you" and they would say, "Aw, I thought so." You know, little stuff to get you started, but once they found out it wasn't bothering you, they would stop. You just have to go with the flow.

The Mitigating Effects of Physical Size

One child welfare professional noted that the physical size of a person affected the amount of the harassment offered. If someone was seen as big enough to take care of himself/herself, he/she was less likely to be harassed.

> On the best day of their life in care, it was pretty terrible, on the best day of their life and on the worst day. it was really horrible. They had to absorb from kids never-ending harassment, from the minute they woke up to the minute they went to sleep. Now, depending on the kid, it depended on how bad it was. I know this sounds absurd, but size also has a lot to do with it. If they are kids who can physically take care of themselves, then, they fare better. But they still get a lot of grief.

Kevin suggested that physical size was a factor in potential abuse and victimization of other gays and lesbians:

> You know you get this cute little guy and if he acts queeny, they just bother him, they pick on him, you know because he's vulnerable and they push him around and call him names and beat on him just for the fun of it. I didn't have that problem, I mean, I'm a pretty big guy, I can be butch if I need to be, so they left me alone. I was able to be pretty tough.

Barb commented on the positive effects of size and additionally identified "attitude" as a positive factor in warding off abuse:

> I really felt that a big part of not being bothered was my size, because I am a big woman, it saved my butt a lot of the time. I had an attitude and I got respect.

Cumulative Effects of Verbal Harassment

Continual verbal harassment erodes one's sense of self-worth, self-esteem, and internal sense of fit. Constant badgering, name-calling, and snide remarks are injurious to one's mental health. The old adage "Sticks and stones can break my bones, but words will never hurt me" is not true. Words can and do hurt. Although several young people reported how the constant harassment wore them down, this narrative from Angelo's interview best illustrates the point:

> One weekend when I went on a home visit my roommate found a copy of *The Advocate* [a gay news magazine], and he passed it all around to the

other guys and they all wrote their comments on it like: "Come to my room and bend over and I'll give it to you." That's when I decided to leave. They had me to the point where I was crying inside, but I wouldn't let them see it. It scared me more than it bothered me. But they never let up. In such a short time they made me feel so bad, it got to me. I was only there for two or three months.

Two adolescents adapted to verbal harassment by seeing that it ended when they took matters into their own hands and put peers in their place. Treg spoke about his need to read [a gay street term for telling someone off] someone who had caused him hurt:

Some of them try to act abusive, but after you read them and show them that you're just not having it . . . then, they don't fuck with you no more! But if you act like one of them scared faggots, I don't like to use that word, but . . . then they fuck with you. They need to give you space and just respect who you are.

Tamil, a sharp-tongued youth from New York, concurred that a good "reading" did some young people the world of good:

When I first came here, honey, they tried that shit with me, calling me a homo and a faggot and all that, but, then those same boys were up knocking on my door late at night. I knew the deal. All I had to do is read them once, real good, and that was that, no more verbal harassment for me. I was just not going for it!

Mike's account is an example of the hurt that can be experienced as one seeks to find a good fit within an environment polluted by verbal harassment:

I get really tired of the harassment, I mean if somebody calls you something it really hurts a lot, even if it's true and even if you're proud of yourself, it really hurts a lot, you don't want to be reminded time and time again, you just want to live your life, you just want to do what you want to do, you don't want people nagging you all the time or asking you a whole bunch of questions, I mean it really gets on your nerves.

The Community

Since group homes and foster homes are located within neighborhoods, there were cases where gays and lesbians reported that some people living in their communities also took part in verbal harassment. Eddie, from New York, recalled the difficulties he encountered while simply walking home from the subway:

> When I was at Partnership House, the neighborhood was all Jamaican and they don't accept gay people. Every day coming home on the subway from school I would get harassed, they would be whispering and yelling out "homo," I mean, there's only so much that you can take. I couldn't be safe at home, I couldn't be safe in the group home or in school, and then, I can't even get from the subway to where I was living? I finally said this is not the place for me.

A New York child welfare professional corroborated the difficulties that gays and lesbians sometimes encounter within their communities:

> This one young boy was taunted and teased so badly in the community that he couldn't even go outside, the kids would chase him. There was an incident where he was molested, it was just horrible, it was just very, very bad and we had a lot of difficulty in the community. Eventually this child developed hallucinations and he had to be re-hospitalized. I mean this child just couldn't even live in the community in peace.

Physical Violence

In many cases, young gays and lesbians worried that verbal threats could escalate into physical violence. When this did happen, many of them left where they were in search of another environment where the possibility was less likely. Gerald, a Trinidadian from a New York agency, recalled that he left placement when the verbal harassment he had been experiencing in his group home turned to hate graffiti on his bedroom walls:

> Kids were always calling me fag and other hurtful things. Once I went to the city on a home visit and when I came back I found written on my wall the words, "Kill Fags." It was around the time that a friend of mine was killed and I thought, "if they killed her imagine what they would do if they found out I was gay."

Gay and lesbian adolescents in out-of-home-care child welfare settings are placed at special risk for violence, not by any inherent factor related to their sexual orientation, but because of the biases, discriminatory behaviors, and inequalities of power in the agencies around them. Accordingly, more than half (52%) of those interviewed believed they were victims of physical violence directly related to their gay/lesbian orientation. Violence that occurred within child welfare agencies was in some cases perpetrated by other young people, in other cases by staff members. For many, physical abuse was seen as the last straw before they "absconded" to the streets. Their experiences resonated with the experiences (Fitzgerald 1996; Holdway and Ray 1992; Janus, Archambault, and Brown, 1995; Meston 1988; Webber 1991; Zide and Cherry 1992) of other young people who exited out-of-home care. For the young people in this study, physical violence was the decisive factor that constituted a poor fit. At this point, many voluntarily fled their placements. Many felt that their very lives depended upon leaving placement.

The stories of these twenty-seven young people are filled with pain. Their narratives chronicle the most heinous accounts of a poor environmental fit. They are stories about rape, violence, and fear.

Family Members

For some young gays and lesbians, the violence they experience begins with their own families. A family frequently reacts with violence toward the news that a child is gay or lesbian (Hetrick and Martin 1987; Hunter and Schaecher 1987). A New York child welfare advocate for children suggested that many families whom he saw in Family Court also participated in the process of physical abuse:

> We just keep seeing kids getting beat up and thrown out of their houses, kids getting beat up by their fathers for being gay, or young lesbians getting sexually abused by male relatives trying to change them so they won't be gay. Or lesbians getting pregnant so they prove they are women. I mean gays and lesbians are different from other minority groups, if a kid is getting beat up because they are gay, who do they go to for services? They usually can't go home and tell why they are getting beat up.

Despite the fact that one of the primary goals in child welfare is to reunite children with their families whenever possible, family reunification was often not seen as an option for gay and lesbian children. One child welfare professional in New York gave this detailed overview of young people's estrangement from their families:

> We have some kids who would tell you the real reason why they left home

and about how they couldn't take it anymore and that their families really gave them a hard time. What I had a chance to see is that when you measure one trauma against another, you realize that all of these kids, with all of their problems, are really about the same. There are differences but it's not so much that it is insurmountable, but they have all been hurt as deeply as the next one. But the big difference is that gay and lesbian kids have no way back. So while we talk about family reunification with somebody because they couldn't take their mother's drinking anymore, or their mother's boyfriend would come in and beat the hell out of them and they couldn't take it anymore. You can refer people like that to counseling and say you can all work this out. But where there was an issue of a kid being homosexual, forget it, and it was so sad, because this kid was like painted into a corner and they needed somewhere they could not only receive validation of their own humanity again, but they needed some way that they could see past the present, they had to learn that their lives were not defined by their sexuality. You cannot define people by their sexuality. Basically the only thing that is different about gay kids in foster care from other kids in foster care is that they just have one more thing hanging over their heads.

The pain adolescents felt in being rejected by their families and then by the system itself overwhelms many, as the narrative of this social worker, from Los Angeles, shows:

Their families are nonexistent. Many of these kids were living at home with their families one day and then after they came out or were found out they got thrown out. They were completely unprepared for that rejection. Can you imagine what is like to be loved and embraced by your family and then in a flash be rejected? It's a terrible, terrible thing for these kids. There's no going back home after that kind of rejection. I've heard gay and lesbian kids say, "I don't come from a single-parent family, I come from a no-parent family—I don't have a family anymore." It is an overwhelmingly sad experience.

Young people recounted numerous stories of physical abuse by family members. Albert recalled how he felt:

When I came out, my stepmother hit me. I had never been hit before. And I just stood there and I was like shocked and then she hit me again and I was just like, why are you hitting me . . . I couldn't believe it. Things were never the same after that. I couldn't deal with it. I kept running away.

Carl, a young Jamaican from a New York group home, vividly recalled this story of familial rejection:

At home my stepfather was physically abusive to me and told my mother that I was gay. When my mother came down from Jamaica and arrived at the airport from New York, she kissed everybody but me. The first thing she said to me was, "we're gonna take you to the doctor"; when I asked why she said, "To see if you is gay!" I said, "Forget it," I wasn't going, and then the relationship even deteriorated further to the point where I just couldn't live in her house anymore. I moved in with my aunt and she accused me of having a relationship with her son, which wasn't true, that's when I left her house and went to Willows.

Accounts from lesbians show that they also endured family violence. As Wilma said:

When my family found out that I was a lesbian, they just went crazy. Even my brothers saw it as a reason to hit on me. My mother watched me constantly. She wouldn't even let me out by myself. We used to get into huge fights about my being gay, real physical—hitting, punching, the works. Finally one day, I just thought, they are never gonna accept me and I left. I couldn't take it anymore, anywhere would have been better than there.

Peers

The negative impact of peer culture within out-of-home-care settings is a well-documented (Mayer et al. 1978; Polsky 1962; Schaefer 1980) and powerful presence for all young people in placement. Peers within the out-of-home-care systems were frequently identified by gay adolescents and casework professionals as active participants in the victimization and violence process. Recalling his first day in care, Wilem said:

The first day I was there though, I got hit in the eye with a milk bottle at breakfast, some kid threw it across the room at me, I literally never knew what hit me. I got treated and when I tried to come back, I was told that I couldn't come back in. Janus House had all drug addicts and you couldn't leave your stuff there, I had to leave my things at the field office, it was safer there than in the group home. I finally got to a point where I started staying at these group homes and I would sleep there during the day and go out all night, which worked well for me.

Many of the most serious attempts at victimizing gays and lesbians occurred during the evening hours when there were fewer staff on duty and when some residents knew that they could take action against anyone who was considered to have stepped out of line. José recalled:

At St. Peter's, they were all bullies there, I was getting beat up all the time, I was terrified at school and where I lived. I slept in the basement in the group home and one night this kid who had been bothering me took my pillow while I was sleeping and tried to suffocate me and then a whole bunch of other guys just started joining in, beating me, throwing stuff at me, I was crying and I was screaming, "Why don't you just kill me, why don't you just kill me?" Because to tell you the truth, right then and there, at that point, I just wanted to die. This all started about me being gay, in fact the kid that they told to beat me up, was one that I was going out with. When I was younger it was worse, I would be sitting watching TV and older guys would come up to me and put their dick in my face, or they would slap my ass, or pinch it . . . I just got to a point that I thought, "I'm just not going to take it anymore."

A common theme expressed throughout these interviews was that those in the peer group who might be questioning their own orientation, or who seemed very invested in hiding, or who were possibly trying to "pass" as heterosexual were often the most abusive. Michelle reported:

I had three kids who used to harass me, the worst ones, and I knew they were gay too, they are all in the life, I see them in the Village, they are in the closet and they are so scared to get bashed that they join in the bashing themselves, they make it so much more violent for the out people.

Some admitted that they too were homophobic before they came out. Fred comments:

It took a while . . . and now I know that I am gay, and that I can get into it, it's all right, at first, even I used to think it was sick when I was about 12 or 11, I used to say that I would hurt a homosexual if he made an approach to me, I would beat him up, you know it's funny to see how you end up, you know? It's really wild, but today I know that it's ok, we're just normal people.

Staff corroborated these accounts, commenting that there was harassment, particularly from peers who are questioning their own sexuality. One New York City social worker said:

There is a lot of harassment, but I think it mostly comes out of fear too. It is some kind of challenge to them and I think it raises a lot of questions in them. The ones who attacked this boy the most, the ones who stabbed him in the back the most, were the ones who have questions with their own orientation and when you ask them openly they say they have a girlfriend, but the girlfriend doesn't even exist. They themselves are struggling with their own sexuality, but they are not willing to talk about it openly and they are afraid to talk about it.

Sexual Favors

Although same-gendered and opposite-gendered sexuality in group care is a reality that most child welfare professionals like to deny (Gochros and Shore 1985), many professionals interviewed for this study made comments suggesting that gay and lesbian adolescents made unwanted sexual advances toward peers. However, several young people's narratives suggest the exact opposite. Several young gays reported that other residents, alleged "heterosexual," tried to proposition them for sexual favors. Tracey recounted his experience of turning down the offer:

> Sometimes guys would proposition you, ask you for sex and if you turned them down they would get all pissed at you and then start saying that you were trying to put the make on them, that's when a lot of the fights would start. Once I got attacked so badly in the cafeteria that I had to go to the hospital. It was a boy who was always trying to get me to have sex with him, but he turned it all around and accused me of trying to have sex with him. It was horrible, they moved me four times to different cottages, but the same thing always happened wherever I went.

Wilem had a similar experience:

> Sometimes it was they were making propositions toward me and I rejected them, then they would try to turn it all around and say that I tried to proposition them. A lot of times that led to a big fight, because I was not going for it, and if I had to, I threw down [fought].

Mike noted that being pressured to give sexual favors could be frightening:

> It was scary, a lot of guys, I was in an all guys group home—they harassed me and asked me to perform oral sex on them and all—it was scary.

Several staff members corroborated these accounts. The following is representative of what many professionals said:

> I think that the straight kids try to set up the gay kids and sometimes even try to entice them and create situations with sexual overtones. I think that

frequently gay kids are used by straight kids to experiment sexually and if the gay kid says no, it's turned around and used against them. Gay kids are expected by straight kids to put out and when they say no, it can be a real problem. Undoubtedly when there is an argument or something, the first words out of a straight child's mouth are "You faggot, you cocksucker," it's a given. "You faggot, you cocksucker," it never has anything to do with being gay, but those are always the words that are spewed forth. When all else fails and you're losing the argument, go for the jugular, get raw.

One professional's comments suggest that gays or lesbians are frequently set up:

With gay kids, the worst is always assumed. You don't have to set them on fire—all you have to do is say that "a gay kid made a pass at me." The staff always believes it. I have had this scenario happen time and time again, they always wanted to discharge the gay youngster based on the accusation, usually from either the most homophobic youngster or a kid who initiated the contact with the gay kid and was rejected.

The Community

The external community that participated in verbal harassment also participated in the physical violence perpetrated against these gays and lesbians. Tracey spoke about his community's violence toward him:

People in the neighborhood where the group home was found out that I was gay because residents had big mouths and oh, boy! I got jumped by the neighborhood. They beat the crap out of me. I couldn't even go to and from school without getting harassed. When I told the staff they would look at me and say, "You can hold your own ground!" I would say, "Against four people?" It was like I always had to shut my mouth and if I was to stand my ground, they would try to kill me. So, I just left.

A New York social worker corroborated the high incidence of community violence, which she identified as occurring particularly in foster homes. She said:

I think that once a child who is gay goes out into the community where the foster parent lives, you're going to have problems—a lot of our foster parents live in the South Bronx and Harlem and you are going to have problems with a homosexual kid in that environment. It's the school and the community where you are going to have the most problems, that's where the problems can come in and they can also get beat up there, it's not always a problem in the home.

As if the violence carried out by their families, by their peers, and by members of their community was not deleterious enough, young people reported that the most demoralizing violence they had to endure was from the staff who were charged with caring for them in their out-of-home-care settings.

Staff

Violence inflicted by staff members was not uncommon. Since staff within child welfare settings have significant power over the lives of the young people under their care, they also have countless opportunities to exploit that power. One child welfare veteran, reflecting on the perceived incidence of institutional abuse, made the following observations:

> Then we send them to places like Mount Laurel to protect them from their families and what happens? They are beaten up there too! Not just by their peers, by the way, but also by the staff who are paid to care for them. So in lots of ways these young people are victimized twice, first by their families and then by the child welfare system.

Both gays/lesbians and professionals interviewed reported that physical abuse carried out by staff was frequent. Sharte, from New York, implied that alleged physical restraints by staff members frequently escalated into episodes of physical violence:

> This one staff member is so homophobic. He and I never got along. We were always getting into these physical confrontations that ended with him restraining me, I guess it never went like it was supposed to go because he was always calling the cops on me and then I'd have to go to the station house, fill out all of this paperwork, and go through these changes. It was really more like an assault than a restraint, a personal vendetta.

Although not all staff people participated in violence this flagrant, those interviewed reported that some staffers played a passive role simply by standing by and allowing the abuse to occur. Jared's account:

> They found out I was gay from one of the workers, I don't know maybe he was against gay people or whatever, but he told them I was gay and when

they came up to me and asked me and the way I said, you know, it offended them and they kept on bothering me and picking on me. But too many boys were picking on me and calling me "faggot," saying "come over here and suck my dick." I started to cry, but they didn't stop. I told staff and they got them to leave me alone until later that night when no staff was around and they started again. One of them threw a pillow at me and said, "You like to suck dick, right?" There was about eight or nine of them and we got into this argument and one of them tried to come after me with a knife saying, "You're a disgrace to our race, I hate homos." I kept waiting for the staff to intervene, but they never came in. When they finally came in, they broke it up, but afterward they said "If you hadn't told people that you were gay, this never would have happened." Then they placed me in this room for two days where I was safe but I was so scared. Then they moved me to another agency.

One professional (Toronto) remarked how gay and lesbian young people were targets of violence:

What comes to mind is the harassment and the fact that gay and lesbian kids are targets for violence. We hear about how some of the other young people make plans to come into this young person's room at night when there's a night shift person on and being terrified to sleep at night because they might be beaten up or they might get caught in the bathroom or jumped by somebody that lives in the group home.

Professional respondents from all three cities corroborated interview accounts of physical abuse over and over again. Calling it the "worst situation I ever ran into," one direct care worker recalled how some residents identifying as straight were allowed—by staff—to sexually use a young gay

I remember in one of my first jobs, where we had this kid who was sleeping with other kids, it was an all-male facility and there was this one kid who everybody used to fuck because he was seen as the gay kid and didn't mind taking it. Workers knew about it, they felt it was okay because if they let this go on, then "we won't have to worry about this with anyone else." Until I got there, they thought this kid didn't really mind. But this kid minded it completely, he was being completely abused, but he felt, well, if he let them do it, then they won't mind me being the only gay kid on campus. It was probably the worst situation I ever ran into.

In their interviews, gays and lesbians frequently complained that they did not feel safe in out-of-home placements. Comments from this professional verified that they had a right to be wary in group care settings:

> Gay kids are scared and they have a right to be. In one case, we had a gay kid tell us that in the middle of the night a group of boys from the group home encircled him and put a gun to his head. They threatened him and told him if he ever told anyone that they would kill him. When we found out, we immediately conducted a room search and found nothing, but a week later when we did another search, we did find a gun. In one of our group homes one of the kids said that he was gay and the other kids said that they were going to have a "blanket party" [that is, when someone rushes in, throws a blanket over the head of the unsuspecting victim, and everyone joins in plummeting the victim]—all of the staff knew this. The staff sanctioned the "blanket party" because a kid was gay. I mean, group homes are hard places to live in, even straight kids can't stand up to the teasing sometimes, so can you imagine what it is like for the gay kids who have no support from their peers or from staff?

Not only were they abused by staff, gays and adolescents were aware that they were not likely to receive help from staff when they brought verbal harassment or physical abuse issues to staff attention. Gerald comments:

> When I told the staff that I just couldn't take it anymore, that all of the guys were picking on me, they said, "Why are they picking on you?" I said, "They're all calling me a faggot and a homo." They said, "Well, you shouldn't have told them that you're gay, what do you expect."

Several staff members corroborated these accounts and remarked that on occasion, staff members sanctioned violence by allowing it to happen:

> I've heard situations where a child care worker sent other kids to really beat them up. We have one kid here who was actually beat up by other kids in his group home because of his orientation. He said to us that workers knew it was happening. They said there was nothing they could do about it. It was actually that there was nothing that they would do about it. There's a big difference.

Comments from many staff members recalled how young people reflected the unequivocal theme: "I couldn't take it anymore," as their credo after an episode or a series of episodes of violence, as this child welfare professional remembered:

> I heard one young man say that when he could no longer take the harassment and the threats of physical abuse from the other residents that we went and told staff. The staff asked, "What are they calling you?" The youngster replied, "you know, a homo, faggot, all that." The staff replied, "Well, you are, aren't you?"

Those at Greatest Risk

Young gays and lesbians identified peers who were seen as gender nonconforming—those perceived as too effeminate or too butch—as at greatest risk of violence. These young people, who may or may not have been gay or lesbian, as gender nonconforming behavior or mannerisms do not necessarily indicate one's sexual orientation, were perceived as gay or lesbian and consequently were treated to all of the abuse which comes along with a stigmatized identity. When one is perceived as gay or lesbian, because of gender nonconforming ways of dressing or mannerisms, one is deprived of using the advantages of hiding. Jason identified the benefit of being able to hide in this reflection:

> I never really had any problem, you know, being gay and being in a group home, because even now I don't really tend to, you know, seem feminine or to, you know, carry myself in a gay manner, um, but I mean, you always hear, like, you know, the residents in group homes talk about gay people like saying how they are weird or, you know, or how they would fuck 'em up or whatever if they were to get approached by one.

Tracey recalled a similar story:

> It was so unfair there the way they treat you and there was this guy that acted more effeminate than I did and he was a closet case and I think people knew . . . they treated this guy like junk and soon they started to treat me like junk and I used to get beat up on by other residents.

A staff member remarked on the maltreatment of the stereotypical "flamboyant" gay male:

> A lot of the gay boys we work with act effeminate or in a flamboyant manner and they stick out. Some of them have said that they couldn't tolerate

the group homes because being gay they were persecuted sexually, physically, and verbally by the other boys. Some of them even catered to that and were willing to be the sexual partner for the boys, almost compulsively sexual, they used to give blow jobs and that sort of thing, but at a certain point, they had enough of that and then hit the street life. Some of them figured if that's what they were doing they might as well get paid for it.

As evidence of the increased level of abuse directly related to gender nonconforming behavior, another professional recalled how one young man she had worked with suffered harassment from his peers:

> We had one boy who was gay and he was very, very good in the group home, however, the other children were making him miserable, he was very effeminate, they were chronically picking on him. He didn't do any approaching of any of the other boys in the group home, and that was not the issue, I think the issue was that he was effeminate.

Rape

The worst cases of staff perpetrating violence, however, were heard from those young people who reported being raped by staff members. Rape is not an uncommon form of violence directed at both lesbians and gay men (Comstock 1991:198–203). Those interviewed for this study were no exception. Of the fifty-four interviewed, four reported actual rapes—three women and one man. Several others reported that they lived in constant fear of this harrowing possibility. In recounting her experience of an attempted raped by a male staff member, Sharice vividly recalled:

> I had a man counselor and he knew about me, you know, about seeing women and all, and one day when everybody else was out on a trip he said I had an appointment with him and said that I had to stay behind. And we was talking and talking and talking, and so he asked me if I had ever been with a man and I was like, no, and then he started to put his hands all over me and you know tried to molest me. When I resisted he started beating me up, but someone came in and stopped him. But he had already beat me up, I had all knots all over my head. He just kept telling me that I was not supposed to be with women, I was supposed to be with men and that this is not the life you is suppose to live. We had to take him to court and everything, he lost his job. Then when I went to another group home, they tried to do that again, and then after that I decided that I would not go to no more group homes.

Wilma, who was raped by a staff member, described her experience:

> I was abused in the group home by the male staff. I would get beat up, and
> you know I got raped in the group home by a staff member, by the custo-
> dian, by a man who worked there, you know, the ones who clean up. When
> I told the counselors they would say "oh, we don't believe you, you proba-
> bly just wanted it, you was probably hot anyway, look at the kind of girl
> you are, 'cause you in here aren't you?" It was just real bad. I ran away a
> lot because I got tired of being raped. I want to say that I don't understand
> why it is that every time in a group home, I see gays get raped more than
> straight people, especially like gay females, but the gay guys also, they get
> raped more than straight people do. I don't know, maybe it's because . . . .
> I just don't understand why I can't even think of an answer to it all, but all
> that I know is that they rape the gay people more, maybe it's because of the
> way that they live their life, maybe it's because they feel that if they get
> raped that they will turn back to the other side or whatever, but, it's always
> the gays that get picked on and I hate that! I'm not saying that straight peo-
> ple don't get raped too, you know, and that's the thing I hate, and I hate
> hearing the guys saying that they got raped in the group homes too. It's just
> terrible, you know, it just terrible the things that people do to you just be-
> cause you want to be happy, you know, it's bad.

Rape was committed by men on these young women as a corrective for
lesbianism. These rapists were under the delusion that if a lesbian had a
sexual experience with one good man (as each believed himself to be),
then their "impediment" would be remedied. The act of rape, one of the
most humiliating experiences that anyone can endure, was also recounted by Ralph:

> The first place I was sent to, I was eight, was in Maples. I was raped there
> by this counselor. He told me that if I told anybody that they would just
> keep me there or put me in another group home. I was there for five months
> and then I ran away, I was tired of being raped, I was repeatedly raped.
> Then I went to a foster home and it was real strict, I left there and went to
> another group home and there somebody tried to set me on fire. I was sleep-
> ing and they put lighter fluid on my bed and threw a match on me, I got
> burned on the leg [he points to an eight-inch burn mark]. The staff didn't
> do nothing, they knew about it, they just moved my bed, but that's staff,
> you know? I didn't feel safe there, you kinda had to sleep with one eye
> open. I finally left. I was tired of that shit.

In an earlier interview, an advocate for gay and lesbian adolescents corroborated the above story, noting that this terrible case of abuse was a catalyst for starting an agency to "protect" gay and lesbian youth. He recalled:

> What I really remember is that there was a kid in a group home who was complaining about harassment and nothing was being done about it and his requests for assistance were being ignored and then the kids in the group home set his bed on fire while he was in it. He was badly scarred. They set his bed on fire with lighter fluid. That was one of the first things that brought us all together. . . we said, this is terrible, but this is not an isolated incident, this is a systematic problem and that incident was the catalyst that helped us to start the Shelter.

These experiences, as with all trauma, caused long-lasting scars of both a physical and psychic nature, as Janet recalled:

> I got beat up a lot because I was gay—the staff actually encouraging it. You got to go through a lot of shit with the group home, inside and out, and with the staff. I eventually got kicked out because the staff was homophobic—one staff member he said he was gonna stick his cock in my crotch to show me what it was like to be with a real man. Male staff would say things like "all you need is a good fuck." I still have nightmares about it.

The Relative Safety of the Streets

The debilitating effects of verbal harassment and physical violence, which embraced the poorest elements of fit, caused more than one half of the young people interviewed to migrate to the relative safety of the streets. Finding life in the group home, foster home, or campus setting to be intolerable, these youth stated that they felt "safer" on the streets than in their out-of-home-care setting. Young people who fled to the streets, or who began to spend more time outside of their group home or foster home, were those who were no longer willing to tolerate the poor fit that was manifest in such settings. Those who declared that they were no longer willing to "take it" defined "it" as sexual or physical abuse or severe psychological and emotional neglect.

Escape from dangerous and even life-threatening conditions, note Bucy and Able-Peterson (1993), is actually a healthy response to intolerable situations. In some cases the violence and alienation that these young people experienced on the streets may be less that what they endured from their families or in some out-of-home-care child welfare settings.

The flight from their families or group homes to the streets does not actually happen in one swift move, but is usually a gradual process that takes place over a period of time. Because they saw that most staff members were unable to be responsive to their needs and because most felt that out-of-home-care settings were unnurturing and hostile environments, these young people felt that they had no option but the streets. Although the streets of any city would hardly seem like a place to find a good fit, of the fifty-four interviewees, fully one half (n=27) indicated that they had lived on the streets at one time or another as an alternative to living in hostile child welfare environment. Tracey best speaks to this experience:

> I couldn't live at home with my family once they found out that I was gay so I was sent to live in a group home. That was worse than living at home. I didn't fit in at home and then I didn't fit in at the group home either. I was living in my fourth group home in like six months and it was horrible. The teasing, the tormenting, the harassment really got to me and one day I just decided that I couldn't take it any more and I left. I had no place to stay, but I didn't even care. I knew that I just couldn't stay one more minute in that group home. I lived with friends, I stayed on people's sofas, I prostituted—I'm not proud of that, but I did what I had to do—to get money to rent a place. I even lived in an abandoned trailer truck with ten other people, slept in railroad tunnels, and anywhere that was warm. As bad as things got on the streets, it was better than the group homes that I had lived in—at least people cared for me on the streets.

Ralph found living on the streets preferable to living at home or in a group home:

> I first went into foster care because I ran away from home, I was fifteen, I was having problems with my parents, some of it had to do with my orientation. I went to a few group homes, Sandlore was all right, but this other one I was in, they were all so homophobic. There was this one counselor there, I couldn't stand him, he used to say, "you faggot" and all that, and it was just his attitude. I could tell he didn't like me very much and it was really hard to live there because the other kids saw him doing that, then they felt that they could do that too, so they made my life there impossible. I left there. I just couldn't take it anymore. From there I lived on the streets, I would rather live on the streets than there. The people are more understanding on the streets. There's no problem. I kept running back and forth to shelters and group homes, but I always left them.

Young people in all three cities noted this phenomenon. In Toronto Jeremey reported:

> I lived in the street for a while; I couldn't live in that place anymore, the
> kids, the staff, the whole experience was horrible. Believe it or not, the
> streets were better.

In Los Angeles, Peter spoke about how he and his sibling, John, had to
live on the streets:

> We spent a couple of weeks on the streets because it was impossible to live
> with our aunts because they said we were going to hell for being gay.

In New York, recalling how he fled the system because it was grinding
him down and because he saw it as unsafe for him, Tracey recounted his
frightening journey:

> The city don't like runaways, but they never paid much attention to me and
> so when I had to, I just left. . . . I used to get beat up by the other residents.
> That's where I had the hardest time and every time I left, the city would
> send me back. I just kept running away and they kept sending me back and
> saying, "work it out." One day one lady at CWA said, "give it thirty days
> and if it still doesn't work out, I'll replace you. Thirty days later I was back
> and she did replace me, that worked for a while, I was there for three years
> and then I had to be replaced again.
>
> At that point I just went to live on the streets. I slept at first on the trains,
> but then I started to sleep at this spot in Penn Station along the Long Island
> Railroad, track 18 or 19, not on the track, but sometimes under the platform,
> where there was a little space, it was dark, but it was a place to sleep.
> Then I went to this place called the Underground, there were about thirty
> or forty people living there, it was an abandoned trailer at 34th Street and
> 11th Avenue. In the winter it was cold there, we kept warm by making a
> fire in a large can inside the trailer, it was ok, but it got pretty smoky there.
> We found food to eat outside of the fancy restaurants. . . It wasn't the greatest
> at the trailer, but it was safe there and no one really bothered you.
>
> I hate to admit it, but I also prostituted myself. I wasn't really one of
> the greatest things, it really wasn't but it was like a lot of us young people
> did it and I had never tried it but it's, it's money! You see some people used
> this money to smoke their lives away but whenever I got this money it was
> to eat. I did it about three times and after the third time, the girl I was
> telling you about, she was telling me stories about how certain hookers or
> male prostitutes or female prostitutes were found hung, heads decapitat-

ed, these were not just fake stories, these were true stories in the paper—
it made me think.

No one ever went to the youth shelter. I had been there before and they
were not so nice to gay and lesbian people because it's predominantly
straight people in there and people always jump you there. All those people do is either call the cops or throw both of you out, which really doesn't
help because then you're out on the street again.

Gerald told a comparable story, noting that his inability to live safely with
his family or in an out-of-home-care setting made him feel so despondent
that he thought about ending his life:

> I left and I couldn't take it anymore. I was on the streets from June to Sep-
> tember 1989. I always realized I shouldn't be on the streets, but I had no
> where else to go. I kept calling my social worker at Hope House to see if
> she could get me another placement. She kept encouraging me to come
> back, but that was only because my youth advocate was calling her to pres-
> sure her. I felt so bad: I felt like I wanted to kill myself, but I saw other peo-
> ple who made it and it made me hopeful.

In many cases, not welcome in their own homes and then finding little or
no acceptance in a group home or foster home, these young people often
felt like they were nobody's children, as Richard noted:

> I just wasn't satisfied where I was. I didn't like it. Some of the places don't
> treat you right. 'Cause you not their child and it's like to me they think, this
> is not my child and I can do anything I want to him. At this one group
> home, the staff said, "Oh, he's gay and he can't be here." They told me that
> God didn't intend for people to be gay and that I should be ashamed of my-
> self listening to gospel music and going to church and praising the Lord and
> all and then I was doing something that was against God. That made me
> feel bad, bad, so I just left there. I couldn't take it, I would rather be on the
> streets than in a place where I wasn't wanted. I didn't let them know I was
> going to leave, I just did.

Sadly, several young people noted that they found a better sense of family on the streets than in a group home. Ralph's remarks represent the
thinking of other young people:

> I was in so many group homes, they were terrible. I couldn't talk about my
> identity, I couldn't be myself, all of the staff were so insensitive, the kids just
> did what they saw the staff doing. One day I just couldn't take it. I left, I

had no where to go, but I literally went to live on the streets. It's sad to say but for the first time I felt like—it's like family on the streets, we are like family on the streets. I guess because we all shared the same experience—lots of my friends on the streets were gay or lesbian and had also been in foster care.

Many left outside-of-home care when they felt unwanted or unwelcome. Maura gave her reasons for leaving:

When I said I was gay, she freaked, she tried to put me in a separate room, she didn't want me near any of the other girls. When some of the girls tried to talk to me she told them to get away from me and when she told the other staff member, she started screaming. At Immaculate Mary, they didn't say anything, but it was damned obvious. I felt that if they couldn't deal with me, then I would just awol. I mean my feeling was, I couldn't live at home because my mother couldn't deal with it, and if the staff in the group home couldn't deal with it either, then why was I bothering sticking around? As soon as I was discriminated against, I awoled. I'd go to the streets if I had to. I mean they were supposed to be helping me with my depression, not telling me I was wrong by being who I was.

Some of the more fortunate banded together with other gays and lesbians to find homes and employment, as well as to provide emotional support for one another. The more resourceful of these young people recreate new family systems, families of choice that sometimes include older lesbians or gays fulfilling the parental roles in an effort to nourish one another with the familial nutriments that they lacked in their biological family systems. Jeremey spoke about the need for family:

I met other people who were like me. Some of us lived together for a while. We'd work, share the rent, and be, you know, be like a little family. It was really nice. We supported one another, we had fights and all, but we resolved them amongst ourselves. We had people of all ages, some younger, some older. We were tight, we were, like I said, like a little family.

Others sought emancipation and moved, often times prematurely, toward independence, like Maria:

When I left the group home I tried to make it on my own, but I didn't have a GED, I didn't have any skills, and all I could do was work in the bathroom of this lesbian bar. It was all right, but I couldn't really deal with the independence of it all. I mean I loved being on my own, but it's hard out there—I didn't really have any support from anyone.

Some young people reported becoming casualties of their unmet needs, abusing alcohol and other substances, engaging in survival prostitution, or becoming involved in other activities in the sex trade industry. Brenda had all of these experiences:

> I'm not proud of it, but I prostituted, I had to. I had friends who said that it was a good way to make money. Since I had no job, no skills, I needed to make money somehow. But it was really scary out there. This one girl who I knew got killed. We all did drugs—lots of them, all types. It was a terrible cycle, we prostituted to make money to rent a room, we did drugs, and then we did it all over again. I was a mess during that period.

Many who have spent time in the sex trade industry or on the streets are already, or will become, HIV-infected (Athey 1991; Hunter and Schaecher 1994; Kruks 1991; Luna 1991). Fred illustrates this point with a disclosure about his own HIV status:

> Yeah, I've seen a lot of friends die from AIDS. I'm HIV positive myself. I got infected because I just didn't care who I slept with, in fact, I'd have to say if I was being honest that I didn't even care if I got AIDS. Things were so fucked up in my life, that I didn't care if I lived or died. I had no family, I had no place to live . . . who cared?

At times, the stress, as evidenced by the above account, was more than many could endure. Some gays and lesbians reportedly attempted suicide (Kournay 1987; Remafedi 1994; Rofes 1983) to escape from the isolation and estrangement, as Wilem recalled:

> I slept with older men so that I had a place to stay at night. Some were nice to me, some were shits. I was high everyday, my life was a mess, I hated myself. I had nothing. I tried to kill myself several times, finally I was hospitalized and then I started to get better.

Clearly the streets are not free from harassment (Seattle Commission on Children and Youth 1988; Victims' Services/Traveler's Aid 1991), but for some, even the streets were preferable to life in the group home as Eddie noted:

I awoled from my first placement because of the harassment I got from the neighborhood, everyday, on my way home from school coming from the subway stop, I was taunted and yelled at by men hanging out in the streets. I was so afraid, I had to get out of that neighborhood. I asked them to get me out of there and then they couldn't find me a placement. Finally they sent me to one of the City group homes. I tried to act real straight and all, but they could still pick me out. I mean this is a thing I have to work on is how I carry myself on the street. When I walked in this group home they were all having a fight and I thought, oh, no. So I took off my earrings, went up to my room, and locked my door. This real big boy, real straight, told me if anybody bothers you, tell me and I will deal with them. I hated it there, I used to pray that I could leave. One day I just couldn't take it anymore, and I left, I went to the streets, stayed in some shelters, lived with friends, it was better than the group home.

Overwhelmingly, child welfare professionals substantiated these accounts. Although many had no idea about how to deal with gay and lesbian young people, many professionals acknowledged that these young people were, as a group, very mistreated by the system. The comments of one professional not only confirmed what these young people had experienced, but also posed several important questions for child welfare professionals to consider:

In the worst scenarios kids are kicked out of their homes, sent to a diagnostic center for a work up, then get sent to a place like Mount Laurel get beat up, then finally they give up and go to the streets. I mean it's horrible. And we are supposed to be in the business of protecting kids? I mean we take kids away from their families and place them within the "safety" of our group homes! Who are we kidding? What are we doing with these kids? No one knows how to work with them, there are no special programs for them, there's no training for child welfare professionals in how to address their needs—there's nothing! What protection do we offer these kids? No other group of adults would tolerate this abuse or maltreatment of their children. And where are our gay and lesbian child welfare professionals? They're hiding too! What a mess! It's a perfect example of institutional abuse.

Raped, beaten up, and living under a virtually constant threat of violence, these fifty-four adolescents have had experiences more like those of convicted felons in a state penitentiary than of what should be expected when placed in out-of-home child welfare systems. Indeed, the fit these young people found was not good. Unable to live with their own families, not welcomed but abused within those settings designed to care for them, caused half of them to flee. Those who rebelled against this hostile environment sought out the relatively safety of the streets over the foster care system. In the words of Jeremey: "it was more like a family than those who were in my group home."

The narratives of these gays and lesbians underscore at least two fundamental kinds of imbalance: (1) the needs of gay and lesbian adolescents are not adequately met by their families or by most out-of-home care settings, and (2) the response of systems designed to provide care have been woefully inadequate in fulfilling their charge. The first imbalance appeared again and again in their narratives as these young people continually sought to find a good fit. The sad reality that families were unwilling or unavailable to care for their children was recalled with bitterness by many. And the fact that child welfare service delivery systems could not properly care for them angered them the most. The lives of young gays and lesbians would be much improved if families learned more about them. Such thoughts of unprejudiced familial response are, of course, fantasies, without the massive reeducation efforts needed to encourage families to support their children regardless of their sexual orientations.

To scrutinize family obligations for gay and lesbian adolescents, without examining the child welfare system's accountability for them, is to minimize the government's responsibility for sustaining and caring for the best interests of all children. Those who espouse the principles of heterocentrism, rather than the principles of good child welfare practice, which proclaims that the system is compelled to care for all children who cannot or should not live at home, share the responsibility and blame for the violence and maltreatment that many of these young people have had to endure.

Verbal harassment was at some point in time an everyday occurrence for 98% of the gay and lesbian young people interviewed for this study. Physical violence inflicted by peers, staff, families, and the community is also commonplace for more than half of them (52%), and led equally as many (50%) to seek the perceived "safety" of the streets.

On hearing these stories it would seem that, where gays and lesbians are concerned, the concept of "caring for" or "protecting" all young people in need of care does not apply. Discrimination, bias, and the absence of written policies appears to have allowed these environments to go unchecked. Excusing the perpetrators for the violence and not holding them accountable for their negative actions victimizes the gay youngster twice: first, by their peers and staff, who are permitted to act on their hate, and second, by the system that silently sanctions the activity by not working to create a more gay/lesbian-affirming environment for all young people to live in.

CHAPTER 5

|A Plan for Transformation|

Exploring what gays and lesbians have to say about their experiences in out-of-home care provides knowledge and suggests a formula for characterizing the meaningful links between these young people and their environments (Hartman and Laird 1987:587). By articulating and rearticulating to others their own narratives and interpretations of their lives, these young people take back the power that was wrested from them by unresponsive environments. As they described, named, pooled, and honored their own stories (Weick 1990), they reconstructed their own identities and reconfigured their fit within nurturing environments.

The life stories collected here vividly depict the tribulations these young people felt as they embarked on a constant search for environments that could provide them with "a good fit." When and if they found a responsive environment, they suspended the search and got on with their lives. Conversely, when and if they found themselves to be negotiating a life within a stress-filled, unnurturing, and hostile environment, they either tried to adapt to that inhospitable environment or moved to the next level.

They searched for a good fit on two tiers: internal and external. On an internal plane, they looked for a fit within the context of their personal identity development; externally, they searched on three levels: within their family systems; within the out-of-home-care child welfare systems; and finally, on the streets where more than half dodged environments that were, for them, the quintessence of a poor fit. They found both positive and negative experiences in the three cities from which the sample was drawn.

The dominant features of a good fit for gay and lesbian adolescents, as evidenced by the data presented here, are threefold: (1) safety from physical violence or verbal harassment; (2) a chance to live within the context of an environment which provides the nutrients necessary for integrating one's gay or lesbian identity into all other areas of one's life without hiding or fear of differential treatment should one decide to disclose his or her gay or lesbian sexual orientation; and (3) the prospect of interacting with adults and peers who were affirming and nurturing of a gay or lesbian sexual orientation. Concurrently, these are all elements of good child welfare practice, and are not necessarily unique to the experience of caring for gay and lesbian adolescents.

What Child Welfare for Gay/Lesbian Adolescents Should Be

To serve gay and lesbian adolescents effectively, the child welfare system must first accept that these adolescents do know that they are gay or lesbian. In denying their existence, child welfare professionals have participated in what Hartman (1991:2) termed "the greatest subjugation of all." Although not all gays/lesbians come into placement because they have had problems within their family systems after their disclosures, child welfare programs must be oriented toward the prevention of out-of-home-care placements. The system must focus on preserving and enhancing family life for gays/lesbians rather than immediately removing them from their homes to "protect" other family members who cannot or will not accept such a sexual orientation.

A system designed to serve gay and lesbian youth must not only have "a historical perspective and a social perspective," as Billingsley and Giovannoni (1972:5–6) claim, but also a historical and social perspective on sexual orientation as well as on race and ethnicity. The gay or lesbian young person must be the central focus of the system rather than the incidental or accidental recipient of services designed and operated for other people. What that means is that child welfare services must be based on the historical experience out of which gay and lesbian adolescents must emerge and within which they are still enmeshed. The difficult realities of these conditions—their destructive and constructive features, their uniqueness, their similarities with those other people—cannot be ignored or presumed.

The social perspective requires that, as gay and lesbian individuals, the network of relationships between them and the various levels of North American society in which they exist, must also be understood within the context of that society's views about them. Gays and lesbians cannot be helped to healthy, functioning lives if they are viewed in isolation or in a limited context. They cannot be helped if they are viewed as deviates who "suffer" from an illness perceived (by some) as a physical, mental, and moral condition. Gays and lesbians must be seen as members of a larger community and as members of their own families; and the relationships between the larger, heterosexual society and what it means to be a gay or lesbian adolescent within society must be explicitly recognized, analyzed, and changed. Appraising the ways in which the various dominant systems of the larger society work together to ignore, augment, or impede the well-being of young gays and lesbians is also vital.

Finally, a gay/lesbian perspective requires that the system be analyzed from the viewpoint of gay/lesbian people. This represents a striking departure from the present operation of child welfare programs, which are designed, administered, and evaluated according to the perspective of heterosexuals, and where the twin myths of homosexual molestation and recruitment continue, despite evidence to the contrary, to be accepted as a fact. There is a need for recognizing, honoring, and enhancing the diversity of society, to enhance the well-being of gay/lesbian adolescents (Boyd-Franklin 1989; Devore and Schlesinger 1987; Greene 1990; Laird 1979; Lum 1986; Sue and Sue 1990; Williams 1992).

The welfare of gay/lesbian adolescents cannot be adequately enhanced as long as the mindless dominance of the larger society, heterocentrically oriented and heterosexually controlled, is unchallenged. The misguidedness of the political system toward gay and lesbian people—their levels of participation, power, and struggle for human rights—is an excellent measure of the bias against them. Pharr (1988:21–23) points out that no institutions, other than those created by lesbians and gays, affirm gay/lesbian identity and offer protection. The affirmation and protection usually afforded automatically to most children and families are rights not guaranteed by child welfare agencies to most gay/lesbian adolescents and their families. Of course, there is some variety; some institutions provide more affirming environmental "fits" for gay/lesbian adolescents than do others. But whether one looks at child welfare, education, health care, religion, culture, law enforcement, the media, or any other dominant system within the larger society, we see heterocentrism at work (Mallon 1994). This force makes gay/lesbian adolescents and their families specially vulnerable to life's challenges.

The dominant child welfare institutions in the United States and Canada continue to exclude openly gay/lesbian young people, even though, despite this exclusion, they are present in all child welfare organizations.

This overt heterocentric discrimination has been replaced by a covert but nonetheless effective heterocentrism in the lack of distribution of services to gay/lesbian adolescents. In cities like New York and Los Angeles, where gay/lesbian people are protected from discrimination by local legislation (but remain unprotected by state laws in New York), the discrimination has officially ceased, but exists nonetheless as services that actually reach gays/lesbians continue to be administered in a toxic form.

The behavioral heterocentrism reflected in the inequities inflicted on gay/lesbian adolescents is accompanied by several manifestations of ideational heterocentrism, which in fact serves to perpetuate and protect the behavioral manifestations. As we have seen, efforts for change specifically for gay/lesbian adolescents have almost always been met with a rationale that absolves those upholding the discrimination. These rationales all rest on some pervasive negative conceptions of gay/lesbian people. Each facet of these rationales reflects a refutation of gays/lesbians and the gay/lesbian experience. And this same denial of their existence pervades the language of child welfare practice. Gay/lesbian adolescents have come to be known in agencies not as gay and lesbian but as "hard to place" and "difficult management cases" (CACS 1993). These negative conceptions are additionally reflected in the almost total absence of gay/lesbian adolescence from child welfare literature, with only a handful of exceptions (Mallon 1992a, 1992b; Malyon 1981; Cates 1987; Sullivan 1994) until the past two decades. The majority of child welfare literature totally eclipses the realities of gay/lesbian children and their families to provide a network of child welfare services.

Why won't child welfare professionals acknowledge the existence of gay/lesbian youth within their own programs? Why don't they develop new and more appropriate services? Why do inequities in the existing service systems still persist? and why, in the face of efforts to overcome discrimination against gay/lesbian youth, has so little effective, manifest change come about?

These efforts, which rise and fall in the level of interest allocated by child welfare authorities according to political pressures or threats of class action law suits, failed because they have not been extreme enough. More specifically, they were not conceived or pursued from a gay/lesbian perspective. They did not grow out of a gay/lesbian experience. In addition, they were not based on recognition that some of the dysfunctions were inherent in the existing system of child welfare services.

The most commonly held assumptions concerning gay/lesbian adolescents and child welfare is that a gay/lesbian adolescent's problems stem from his/her negatively valued identity, and that his/her resolutions lie in the institutions of the larger heterosexual society. The reverse interpretation is the more sound one. The fallaciousness of the supposition that the resources for gay/lesbian adolescents lie in the heterosexual society is one of the most fundamental obstacles to that should be changed. The entire child welfare system seems presently predicated on this erroneous assumption. The major sources of power and control over the distribution of child welfare services are heterosexual; but the resources themselves— the nurturance, the sustenance, and the affection—are in gay and lesbian people. It is time, I think, that those who hold control over these resources should turn them over to gays/lesbians or their allies who are trained to administer programs and provide care for children based on sound judgment.

What then should be the direction for transforming child welfare for gay/lesbian adolescents and their families? The answer to this question does not rest with child welfare staff, as there have been so few of them who have ever addressed these issues. The answer, once again, lies with the true experts—the gay/lesbian young people who have experienced life in the out-of-home-care systems in the United States and Canada and who have survived.

Those fifty-four young people interviewed for this study had a lot to say about what needed to be done to improve child welfare services for young gays/lesbians. They had distinct and authoritative recommendations for child welfare professionals interested in working toward the attainment of a better fit between themselves and their environments. The matters most in need of corrective action were issues that exposed the most impoverished child welfare environments.

Their comments were corroborated by many of the ninety-six child welfare professionals interviewed and fall into two broad categories of needed social change. The first are external changes—changes in the character, structure, and operation of the child welfare systems. Concomitantly, internal changes are also necessary. Agencies must be specifically conceived, designed, controlled, and managed by members of the adult gay/lesbian community.

How then can we move toward changing this system and at the same time develop viable gay/lesbian organizations to serve these needs more effectively? The first step is to recognize that today's child welfare organizations were not conceived or structured to be relevant to gay/lesbian adolescents or their families. Most child welfare programs were developed long before the notion of self-identified gay/lesbian adolescents was ever imagined. The separation of group homes, congregate care settings, and foster homes into programs for males and females, in an attempt to extinguish sexual activity, creates desexualized environments to insure that agencies keep the boys and girls apart (Murphy 1981:27–29). The segregation of the sexes, combined with official silence regarding all forms of sexuality, inevitably breeds ignorance and misinformation regarding this important aspect of life. Consequently, by their makeup they fashioned a poor fit for gay/lesbian adolescents and their families. This lack of fit arises from a complex interplay of the forces of heterocentrism, professional political correctness, religious and cultural biases, and child welfare bureaucracy.

Heterocentrism

Individuals who create, design, manage, and sustain child welfare programs participate in a process of corrective education. The purpose of such instruction is to place gays/lesbians into a more authentic and affirmative perspective. The pedagogy of such learning calls for those who educate to consciously and deftly weave together the individual threads of knowledge-building, skills-development, and attitudinal elements into one seamless pattern. The need for such education was urged by the overwhelming majority of both adolescents (88%) and professionals (75%). One young person said:

> They need to have staff who have been trained in diversity issues, including gay and lesbian issues, and they need to be more sensitive. I mean you get put into care because you get thrown out of your own home and then you get put in a place where they can't deal with you either? Where can you go? Staffs need to be more sensitized.

The reflections of most professional staff members parallel that recommendation.

> I think that definitely I would have every foster care agency attend a mandatory training on diversity: lesbian, gay, transgender kids, immediately and put that into a training that they have to have once a year or every time a

new person comes on staff. It has to be mandatory, no ifs, ands, or buts about it.

Effective reeducation efforts cannot be "a one shot deal." Education programs must be comprehensive, objective, and professionally based, with a focus on child welfare policy and practice. This kind of instruction has been absent from both our child welfare training curriculums and academic training.

> I know that they didn't teach about gays and lesbians when I was in social work school. I think we need to do a whole lot more around this issue, I mean, you know there is this whole thing about cultural sensitivity, but I don't hear anyone talking about being sensitive to the gay and lesbian population. It's not a talked-about population because child welfare is homophobic. If you don't talk about it, then you don't deal with it. I don't think that there is representation of the gay and lesbian population we serve. Is the child welfare administration population representative of the gay and lesbian community? No. I think that the child welfare field is by and large homophobic. Sometimes I get so angry when I hear people say—"Oh, it's so much better for gays and lesbians nowadays, people are so much more open," but it's just not true.

A commitment is required from the top level administrators, from the boards and executive directors of agencies to line child welfare workers. Ongoing education and training for all levels of child welfare personnel, including foster parents, are necessary for stimulating the development of appropriate child welfare services for gay/lesbian youths. This process must begin with the top levels and then filter on down to others in the agency. Instructors must be gay and lesbian child welfare professionals or heterosexual allies and, when appropriate, gay and lesbian young people, who can be given opportunities to be the true experts.

Child welfare professionals need to learn new concepts about gay and lesbian identity. They must learn to differentiate myth from fact, master the language and vocabulary that one needs to provide competent practice for this population, and address their own biases and fears about gay and lesbian people. Families also need to participate in such educational efforts in community-based agencies as part of placement prevention and family preservation efforts.

The gay and lesbian communities must be understood in the context of oppressed people who have struggled for acceptance under the weight of stigmatization that is similar to, and yet uniquely different from, the experience of other oppressed people. One fundamental requirement is the abandonment of two important misconceptions about gays/lesbians that still recur. One conviction is that gay/lesbian people are sick and as such should be treated by professionals as thought they are exhibiting pathology, and second is the bias that gay/lesbian people are immoral. Both views are negative and reflective of the heterocentric thinking and paternalism underlying the child welfare system in both Canada and the United States.

Finally, a remedial education program must help professionals to develop more realistic and positive conceptions of the gay and lesbian communities as they function within the larger heterosexual society. The myths of molestation, the most heinous of myths about gay and lesbian people, the falsehood that attempts to segregate and isolate gay and lesbian people from children must be directly engaged. Addressing this issue will make it possible for gay men and lesbians who are child welfare professionals to come out and act as adult role models for younger lesbians and gay males. The work of de Young, (1982), Groth (1978), Groth and Birnbaum (1978), and Newton (1978) rigorously and definitively asserts that the majority of child molestation occurs by heterosexual men who are known to one or more of the family members. The equally erroneous myth of "recruitment" (Mallon 1994, 1995) of young people must also be directly confronted in order to overcome obstacles to providing competent services to young gays/lesbians and their families. Clinical theories that view homosexuality in developmentally pejorative terms and moralistic arguments must also be challenged, so that they can be diffused and answered (Saperstein 1981).

Those in charge of caring for adolescents and designing programs to meet their needs must begin to consider the particular needs of gays/lesbians. Their needs must be considered within the context of gay/lesbian identity and life rather than clinging to a heterocentric perspective that is as faulty for young gays/lesbians as it would be to view young heterosexuals in a homosexual context. The heterocentric perspective focuses its concern on the child welfare structure rather than on the function of gay/lesbian identity for adolescents. This perspective ignores the need for the child welfare system to change itself to fit the needs of gay/lesbian adolescents and their families, and instead implies that families and gay/lesbian adolescents should change themselves to fit the child welfare system.

The fundamental change that must come about if heterocentrism is to be eliminated in child welfare is a sharing and, at some points, a surrender of power and control in support of child welfare professionals from the gay/lesbian population. Gay/lesbian adults, like the people of color communities before them, need to decide on the optimal situation for gay/lesbian adolescents. But gay/lesbian professionals cannot share in this power if they themselves remain in the closet. Many gay/lesbian professionals in child welfare have for too long been so concerned with hiding themselves that they have not been able to be true collaborators in the process of caring for gay and lesbian young people. Heterosexually oriented professionals, even those who are sensitized, cannot be substituted for gay/lesbian adults who share the actual experiences of growing up on the margins of society with these young people. Gay and lesbian professionals, indispensable in this process, must free themselves from the closets where they have been disguised within their heterosexual privilege and speak out on behalf of gay/lesbian youth. Those professionals, who do not professionally come out, deny young people the opportunity to see positive adult role models. Gay/lesbian professionals who hide must also share a responsibility for the institutional abuses inflicted on these young people—their silence makes them collaborators in the process.

Although it is probable that gay/lesbian staff are caught up in the same system of hiding as are the young people with whom they work, until these professionals overcome their own fears and insecurities, only a few gay/lesbian young people will find a good fit; the majority, however, will find a fit that is poor. Some will be raped, beaten, and almost all are assured of being verbally harassed. Still others will be denied services, live in loneliness, be thrown out of their foster homes, and feel the isolation that comes from believing that maybe you are the only one who feels the way you do.

Putting Principles Into Practice

Several young people and their gay/lesbian professional counterparts noted that those educating professionals about heterocentrism needed more than just training—they needed a complementary experiential component:

> You can educate them, you can give them lots of book knowledge and they can say, "Wow I'm really enlightened and my eyes are opened up!" But it's another thing if you put the person who is gay in front of them, then that's when you see all of the fears click in. Agencies really need staff members who are thoroughly trained in what gay and lesbian kids are going through.

Agencies need staff members, preferably gay and lesbian ones, who can model behaviors for them, staff whom they can watch and see what works and what doesn't. You can't just go up to a kid and say: "Are you gay?" That's what a lot of them do, and then they report back that the kid is not gay because they asked them and they told them no. It's a disgrace, but they just don't know any better. Training helps, but there are many other issues that need to be addressed also. A lot of times kids don't feel like they get that from their agencies because they are witnesses to the agency's own fears and issues about gay and lesbian people.

Heterocentrism, although unexpressed outwardly because of the social consequences associated with overt professional bias, frequently diverts this affliction to an underground course. One professional identified this state of mind and called it what it was:

I think that there is a huge gap between the way things are supposed to be and the way that things really are in most foster care agencies. The way things are supposed to be is that we take the traditional, politically correct position with regards to gay and lesbian issues. However, it really has little to do with what is really going on here. What really goes on here is the law of the streets and often that's not very hospitable to gay and lesbian kids, if organizations address those issues and that is not a gay issue, that is an issue of understanding that the informal organizational structure rules the day in most of these agencies. And if we can somehow reduce the gap between the manual and what we really do around here, then we might be able to address those issues better along with a slew of other issues.

The work of several authors (De Crescenzo 1985; Gramick 1983; Gochros 1995; Hartman 1993; Hudson and Ricketts 1980; Tievsky 1988; Wisniewski and Toomey 1987) also present evidence that antigay and antilesbian discrimination is present within the social work profession and point to ambivalence about homosexuality among social workers. Even in mainstream agencies where there is a high level of sensitivity toward responding to the needs of gay and lesbian young people, staff members still noted that many of their colleagues responded in an antigay and antilesbian manner.

Most people have no idea! I mean it's because of the homophobia! I mean homophobia is so rampant in these places and there is a heterosexual assumption. Most professional staff know that they are not supposed to be homophobic, so they try to mask it, but it's just as plain as day. A kid walks in and there is a heterosexual assumption for this kid. And they are going to be there for that kid, and that's all that a gay kid needs too, somebody to be there for them. Someone who has accurate information about them though. Not somebody who is going to get all bent out of shape when Billy says he has these feelings for Johnny or Mary says she got it for Jane. They need people who won't get all bent out of shape, they need people who know how to deal with gay kids. They don't need staff members who make believe that everything is fine, but inside cannot deal with gay and lesbian people. It shows when people are uncomfortable and the kids know it too.

Despite educational efforts, it will still be hard to convince professionals that their personal values about homosexuality prevent them from serving gay/lesbian adolescents. There needs to be not only a realistic set of standards but a distinct one that emanates from their experiences and lives. Such standards can only be adopted when gay/lesbian adolescents are treated equally with heterosexually oriented adolescents. The issues of equality were among the most dominant themes brought to light by young people when asked what elements were imperative for improving child welfare environments. Reflecting on this perceived sense of inequality, one young woman said:

> I feel that there should not be discrimination against anybody just because you're gay or you're straight, I feel that they shouldn't treat you differently just because you want to live your life. They should just treat everybody equal, because they are still human beings. They fail to realize that because you want to be with your same sex. I know that the counselors in my group home feel that every man should be with a woman and that every woman should be with a man, and that two people of the same sex should not be together and that's why they felt that I was wrong. I just feel that they should change that, they shouldn't treat anybody differently.

The impressions of a second young person echoed the call for equal treatment and pointed out the double standards that existed for young gays/lesbians in child welfare environments:

> Gay and lesbian kids need to be treated like everybody else, we are all the same, we just have different sexual orientations and they just don't understand that. I mean there are different rules for the gay kids, if you're gay you have to do this, I mean at the interview they said to me, "We don't have no sex in here you know." I said, "Hey, I'm not coming here for sex, do you tell this to other people too?" and he just ignored me and said, "Next question." I mean they have different questions if you are gay, it's like they are

warning you before you even get there, I thought, "I bet you don't tell that to the other people," it makes you feel uncomfortable. At first when you move in you don't feel comfortable, you always think that people are watching you.

To impose heterosexual standards on gay and lesbian adolescents is not equality, but a blatant form of insensitivity at best, and heterocentrism at worst.

Religion, Race, and Culture

Many of those interviewed felt that sectarianism and bias were inherent within the cultural mores of some countries and thought this to be particularly true in Jamaica and several other Caribbean countries. A commonly held notion that gays/lesbians are sinners and immoral, and in some cases deserving of punishment, has a toxic effect on them and their families. Although rigid sectarianism historically may have served the needs of some heterosexually oriented families in Jewish, Catholic, Protestant, and Muslim agencies, it is a major obstacle to meeting the needs of gay/lesbian adolescents and their families.

Child Welfare Bureaucracy

Multilevel statewide authorities responsible for child welfare licensing and promulgation of rules, which govern eligibility to maintaining child welfare environments, constitute and create impediments for gay/lesbian adolescents. These barriers existed with full potency in New York and California. Programs in Canada, however, were backed by legislation that mandated equal treatment. In New York and California, young people and professionals identified, over and over again, the difficulties they had in convincing state social services officials of the unique needs of gay/lesbian adolescents.

I brought them case records, I brought them documentation, I gave them reading materials, I offered to provide training—for free! They never took advantage of anything that I offered. It was like it was just an issue which they were not going to deal with. We even had a task force to look at the issues which related to gay and lesbian young people and they reluctantly attended two of the six meetings and refused to sign on when the document was completed.

Even when staff were successful in persuading social service officials to open specialized group and foster homes, these homes were more closely monitored than others, and state administrators continued to behave and to respond in heterocentric ways.

> I like being here, but one of the things that I hate about this place is that they are always keeping a very close eye on you. They have to because the State people from licensing are always monitoring us, checking on us and trying to make sure that we are doing what we are supposed to do. I never saw the State monitor other agencies, as much as I have seen them monitor this one and I have been in eight other agencies.

Essentially, these bureaucracies are designed expressly to care for the needs of heterosexual adolescents. Another is that serving the needs of young gays and lesbians is a potentially volatile political problem. Staff reluctance to engage in discussions about adolescents and sexuality of any type expand the lack of responsiveness.

> When we deal with heterosexual kids, we're dealing with kids who have come in abandoned in lots of ways, with terrible abandonment issues. Some of them have been abused not only emotionally, but physically, and we're here to help them develop self-esteem so that when they leave our group homes they're going to be healthy well-adjusted young people going off to college, we hope, that they will do better than when they came in. But what we do for the gay kids is not the same: the message is, "We're going to change you to be like us. And if you don't fit that model, you're not worth saving because we'll let you leave here, if you can't do it our way, goodbye." So in a way they are twice abandoned, first by their parents and then by the child welfare system.

Three Systems of Child Welfare Agencies

We need to abandon the concept of a single heterosexually conceived, heterosexually dominated, and heterosexually administered system of child welfare. A diverse conception of child welfare services and the development of gay and lesbian affirming organizations is needed. Child welfare needs to reform, revise, and build on existing strengths to develop a nonsectarian trinity of service delivery systems: (1) a mainstream system of voluntary child welfare services, like the best of child welfare agencies currently in existence; (2) a system of public agencies which, while operating to serve the needs of all children, can effectively address the needs of gay/lesbian adolescents and their families; and (3) a gay/lesbian system of child welfare services to serve gay/lesbian adolescents and their families in a distinctive way.

Mainstream Voluntary Agencies

Green Chimneys Children's Services, initially designed to meet the needs of groups of heterosexually oriented children and youth, is an excellent example of a mainstreamed child welfare agency. The agency, established in 1947, was conceived, designed, and administered by heterosexually oriented professionals. They received financing from private sources to fund their efforts; however, public monies are a major source of support of all of their programs. The agency recognized the unmet need and has a history of assuming professional risks to diversify service delivery to children and families.

In 1987, the agency began to hire openly gay and lesbian child welfare professionals whose commitment to gay/lesbian adolescents was of a novel quality. These professionals were comfortable working with gay/lesbian adolescents, and began openly to address issues, challenge heterocentric policies, and design programs that insured a better fit for gays/lesbians and their families. The agency's culture, previously heterosexually oriented, began a process of transformation as the staff openly welcomed gay and lesbian adolescents into their array of diversity. In reflecting on this transformational process, one professional from that program made these observations:

> We just decided that we had gay kids and that we did good work with them and we would continue to provide care for them. We made a conscious decision not to discriminate. Initially, we were referred and accepted a number of self-identified gay kids; their orientation was not the issue, their needs fit the mission of the program and they were accepted. Then we began to earn a reputation for being an agency which would take gay kids and then we started to get calls for every gay kid that came through the system whether they were appropriate for the program or not. We ran into a real ethical dilemma, if we took the youngster who was not appropriate for the service we offered, it may not be in that child's best interest; but if we didn't take the child he went from overnight to overnight and was harassed,

bullied, and quite possibly beaten. In most cases, we'd opt to take the gay child to offer protection and to provide them with a safe home. CWA field workers, placement workers, and then court social workers, children's rights advocates, and a whole array of agencies, including gay and lesbian advocacy organizations, would even call us for placements. Our openness to accepting gay kids was unfortunately not the norm.

If mainstream voluntary child welfare agencies are going to make a meaningful contribution and provide a better fit for gay/lesbian adolescents they must be willing to change. Key characteristics of these programs must reflect flexibility in design, commitment, and caring on the part of staff, provision of basic necessities in addition to services, and innovation in service delivery (Schorr 1988). In transforming themselves from heterocentric institutions to inclusive environments that affirm and recognize the uniqueness of gay/lesbian adolescents, agencies like Green Chimneys must confront the heterocentrism in their conceptions of gays and lesbians. This entails a process of discernment in scrutinizing their own organizational functions, in examining their boards and policy-making bodies, in reviewing the openness of their staff members toward issues of sexual orientation and in evaluating their relationship to the gay and lesbian communities.

Although Green Chimneys was instrumental in developing effective programs, system-wide impediments continue in New York City. The obstacles to these changes include: (1) lack of support and open resistance by contract agencies to create sustaining and affirming environments for gay/lesbian adolescents; (2) unwillingness on the part of agencies to transform and to permit their organizational cultures to bend to new service needs; (3) the fear that agencies will be discriminated against by funding sources if they are known to respond to the needs of gay/lesbian adolescents; and (4) the almost complete lack of responsiveness and the manifest disinterest on the part of the New York State Department of Social Services to addressing the needs of gay/lesbian adolescents and their families.

Public Agencies

The public welfare system is mandated by law to care for all children. In this study, there were no public agencies that specifically considered the needs of gay/lesbian adolescents. The only area where there seemed to exist a public agency close to a model of a private one was in the Province of Ontario, in the city of Toronto. The Children's Aid Society (CAS) of

Metropolitan Toronto is one public agency that has shown tremendous potential for meeting the needs of gay/lesbian adolescents and their families. The CAS is one of the largest child welfare organizations in North America. The agency serves Canada's largest city, which is also Canada's corporate and cultural capital. Metropolitan Toronto is one of the world's most diverse cities (CASMT 1995a).

In Canada, child welfare services are organized at a provincial level and delivered at a provincial level by independent children's aid societies across the country (Trocme, McPhee, and Kwok 1996:565). Guided by the Child and Family Services Act of 1984, the agency is legislatively mandated to insure the safety and protection of children under the age of 16, although court-ordered exceptions are frequently made for children up to age 18. A child in care is the responsibility of the agency until he or she reaches the age of 18 or is adopted. Some adolescents who are pursuing an education or who have special needs stay in extended care until the age of 21.

The Children's Aid Society of Metropolitan Toronto is a nonprofit corporation, governed by a voluntary board of directors. The agency is funded jointly by Ontario and the municipality of Metropolitan Toronto and is one of the few child welfare organizations that have tackled the issue of meeting the needs of gay/lesbian adolescents head-on.

Initially stimulated by an amendment to the Human Rights Code in 1986, which included sexual orientation, the Children's Aid Society framed issues of sexual orientation as another aspect of diversity. The effort caucused with other gay/lesbian staff, steering committees developed with youth, members of gay/lesbian community reflected diversity, including straight people. The focus was not exclusively on gay/lesbian rights, but on children's rights to live in environments that are nurturing, affirming, and that constitute a good fit.

As part of this collaboration, the CAS joined forces with several key constituencies including gay and lesbian youth, foster parents, staff from the Central Toronto Youth Services, and other community partners. Consequently, this organization waged an effective campaign against antigay and lesbian discrimination in their child welfare system. The result of their efforts was a report (CASMT 1995b) that made 38 recommendations for transforming public child welfare environments. This report outlined four key systemic barriers that needed to be overcome before child welfare agencies could begin to deliver equitable, accessible, and quality services: invisibility, pathologization, tolerance of antilesbian/gay behavior, and the denial of same-gendered relationships. Four effective

approaches were offered in this report: the need for professional development; the need to reform agency policies; the development of programs
and services; and efforts to advocate on behalf of gay and lesbian young
people (Mc Cullagh 1995; 10–11; O'Brien, Travers, and Bell 1993).

Reflecting on the public organizations responsive to gay and lesbian
young people, one program administrator offered the following reflections:

Most youth are cared for by heterosexual care providers because most
agencies have a policy to exclude gay and lesbian foster parents. Gay and
lesbian young people hide, and in some cases it leads to placement break-
downs. We realized that we needed to make truly systematic change so that
the changes were not just associated with me because I am a gay man and
because I worked toward effecting these changes. I wanted to be sure that
when I walk out of here that the changes stick. One of the first things that
we emphasized was visibility. It was right up in front. We had an entire issue
of the agency newspaper dedicated to gay and lesbian issues. We have a big
poster placed right up in our main waiting room that sends the message that
this is a safe place. We have the *Pink Pages* on a table in the waiting room.
When the poster first went up, it got ripped down and I just kept putting it
up. Finally it stayed. These visible signs are so important for gay and lesbian young people. They signal acceptance. Once, one of my workers had
a client who was flipping through the *Pink Pages* on a table, a new client,
she sat in that waiting room transfixed by the poster and within 30 minutes,
she came out to her worker.

It was our responsibility to help staff and clients recognize that this is an
issue. If we're serious about recruiting foster homes for gay and lesbian
adolescents, then we need to go into the community—we need to go into
the community—we should have a booth on Gay Pride Day—but many
staff members still have the media image of lesbians with their breasts bared
and gay men with rings in their nipples.

It has taken us two years of meetings, training, and hard work. I respect
the work of gay and lesbian specific agencies but in the long run I am interested in making mainstream agencies accountable to gay and lesbian
young people. Support groups for gay and lesbian youth in care is great, but
you need to make changes in mainstream and public agencies if you want
to make sustained changes. We have a long way to go, but I think that we
have made some very significant headway. In some ways I don't think that
we have the same magnitude of problems that you have in the States with
gay and lesbian issues.

Responding to the need for a separate home that emerged from the
voices of young people and from the findings of the above-mentioned

study, in January 1995 CAS opened a new program called LIFE House, in Toronto. It is a residential program designed specifically to meet the requirements of some of the lesbian, gay, and bisexual youth in the agency's care, who felt they had to hide or, even worse, deny their identity in order to "fit in."

Public agencies that wish to make a contribution to gay and lesbian adolescents must become less heterocentric in their conception and more responsive to the needs of their gay/lesbian clients. As was the case with mainstream voluntary child welfare agencies, public agencies must be safe places for gay and lesbian child welfare professionals to be open about their orientation, as their participation in this process is a key to its success. Additionally, public agencies must be become the enabling mechanism for carrying out the decisions affecting gay/lesbian adolescents and their families. The fact that only nine states (California, Connecticut, Hawaii, Massachusetts, Minnesota, New Jersey, Rhode Island, Vermont, Wisconsin), and the District of Columbia, have statewide legislation protecting gays and lesbians from legal discrimination further impedes this process (pers. corr. Human Rights Campaign, July 1996).

Gay and Lesbian Agencies

The major commitment of some public and private agencies is for heterosexually oriented adolescents and their families. Therefore, a strong need exists for specifically gay and lesbian conceived, designed, managed, and staffed agencies. Such a system, the only one of its kind in the United States, exists in the form of the Gay and Lesbian Adolescent Social Services—GLASS—in Los Angeles. GLASS provides group homes for gay, lesbian, bisexual, transgendered, transvestite, and HIV positive adolescents. Gay and lesbian interviewees overwhelming agreed that gay and lesbian group homes would be positive environments from them.

> Like I said before, an all-gay-and-lesbian group home would be great, but secondly I think that they need to be more strict about harassment, I mean when somebody calls you something it really hurts a lot, even if it's true and even if you're proud of yourself, it really hurts a lot, you don't want to be reminded time and time again, you just want to live your life, you just want to do what you want to do, you don't want people nagging you all the time, or asking you a whole bunch of questions. In a gay and lesbian group home I think that you would be more free to talk about what you do. I mean where I live now I'm not free to talk about what I do. When all of the other kids are talking and saying that they were with their girls and they were

doing this or that, I can't just say, Oh, I was with my guy and we were doing this. If it was an all gay group home, it would be different. I mean I can't be free in my group home. I can't say what I do with my gay friends. I really keep it a secret. I keep what I do with my friends a secret. I mean it's not a secret that I am gay, but what I do is secret because there's no one I can share it with.

Another young person made a case for a group home with both gay/lesbian and heterosexual young people describing the benefits of such an approach:

There needs to be a gay group home, or there needs to be a group home which is willing to devote at least part of the population to gay kids. Mixed populations can also work under the right conditions. Peers can sometimes be the best trainers. I know from personal experience that you can have gay kids and straight kids living in the same house, but I know that it doesn't happen automatically. It requires very careful negotiation. You really need to help kids work through their feelings for each other. A lot of the gay kids believed that the straight kids could accept them. Then you get the regular adolescent stuff that comes in, people putting each other down, gay kids who are convinced that straight kids can be flipped. If you ever talk to a straight kid about why he gets along with his gay roommate, you will find that at some point along the way he was probably deprogrammed about the homophobia. Having gay staff is also important, not closeted gay people, people who are out. It's necessary that the staff be out otherwise you give terrible mixed messages.

In addition, GLASS is also a licensed foster family agency for gay and lesbian adolescents as well as for infants, toddlers, and young children who have been abandoned, abused, and neglected.

Despite the fact that, back in 1979, Governor Jerry Brown had signed an Executive Order preventing social services agencies from denying services to young gays and lesbians, youth-serving agencies in California still searched for the next five years for any way that they could effortlessly handle these youth. Their answer appeared in 1984, when Teresa De Crescenzo founded the GLASS program. Her career as a social worker and probation officer gave her a firsthand experience of what most young gays and lesbians faced in mainstream and publicly funded child welfare agencies. In 1985, shortly after incorporation as a city, West Hollywood City Council voted to grant GLASS start-up funding in the amount of $55,000 to set up a six-bed licensed group home. Financing was difficult, some in the community responded negatively and, come election time, politicians who originally supported the effort came under fire for their support. But the neonate agency survived.

By 1987, with the demand for child welfare placements increasing, the Los Angeles County Department of Probation asked the organization to open a second facility with a grant of $45,000. By this point GLASS had already developed a solid reputation in the community. The agency also responded to the call to provide effective residential programming for HIV-infected youths. At the time when this subgroup was added to the organizations mission statement, HIV was seen as a gay disease. At present, the majority of HIV-positive youth living in GLASS programs are heterosexual (Greeley 1994:114–16).

In 1989, the agency expanded its mission to include foster care and initiated a program that recruited, screened, trained, certified, and supervised foster parents. Although this agency's specific mission is to provide care for gay and lesbian adolescents in five group homes and in 140 foster homes, it does not discriminate against heterosexually oriented young people who live in the Los Angeles area. The agency employs gay/lesbian and heterosexual staff with special skills (they are usually people with a gay or lesbian sibling or family member). The board of directors is also representative of the client-base. In many respects, GLASS is just like other child welfare agencies, but the key differentiating significance in these agencies, which makes them gay- and lesbian-affirming, is that it was conceived, designed, and key decisions were made by gay and lesbian child welfare professionals.

GLASS's group homes and foster homes are in an excellent position to be innovative in meeting the needs of gay/lesbian adolescents and their families. Although the agency is licensed and monitored by the State of California Department of Social Services, it is able to set its own standards for caring for those in its charge. What also makes GLASS unique is that it is one child welfare organizations that does not have to contend with heterocentrism, professional political correctness, religious or cultural biases, or child welfare bureaucracy, at least from within its ranks, but it most certainly must cope with these obstacles on an external plane. One worker from GLASS made this comment:

> Our staff really cares for the kids that we work with. That's a big difference. Most of the people who work for GLASS are invested in it. If they are not gay they have a family member or someone. A lot of people in power

however still think gay and lesbian kids should be changed and they will not send them to gay placements. They usually send them to other placements and they don't work there, because they don't fit in those placements. They eventually send them to us.

A central theme in the organizing of the GLASS program is that the agency is first and foremost a child welfare organization run by and for gay and lesbian people. It is an organization that has as its central mission to work with gay and lesbian adolescents and their families within the context of a child welfare environment.

The mainstream voluntary child welfare agencies, along with the public child welfare organizations, all have to continue to work toward creating environments that are affirming and sustaining for lesbians and gays. At the same time, these systems need the support and good counsel of those openly gay and lesbian child welfare professionals who can provide them with an expertise they do not now possess. One professional's comments about the system made her bristle as she reflected on the inadequacies:

> There are a lot of professionals in the system who are lesbian or gay who are out, who need to say "I'm out," and who need to help out here and say, "Let's design something for these young people." Let's make sure that something is convened, not just some goddamn committee, and let's find foster care agencies who really give horrendous treatment for lesbian and gay youth and let's do some type of real study. Not that crap that was sent out in June to ask questions that was bullshit. I saw that and I started laughing, we need to do a real assessment of what's going on out there with gay and lesbian youth in the system. If we are saying that there are 55,000 kids in foster care, then there a hell of a lot, who potentially could be gay and lesbian. They need to give young people the sort of environment where they need to grow healthily and to be able to advance whatever skills they have, that would be my main push.

The need for gay/lesbian child welfare agencies should not be interpreted as a mandate for heterosexual child welfare professionals to design and impose them on the gay/lesbian community. These agencies must be designed and formulated by gay/lesbian professionals, and the role of heterosexually oriented agencies is to encourage and support them in some various ways.

To be clear, all urban areas with gay and lesbian communities need all three types of organizations to meet the needs of gay and lesbian adolescents. Any one of these systems alone cannot respond to the needs, but these three models offer environments which can sustain and nurture young people, and provide a sense of fit.

But, in addition to making changes in the out-of-home-care systems, comprehensive and intensive efforts should be made to keep gay and lesbian adolescents in their own homes. Viewed ecologically, both assessment and intervention must focus primarily on the goodness of fit (Germain and Gitterman 1980, 1996) between the adolescent and those other systems with which he or she is in transaction, the most central of which, in this case, is the family. Many of the issues that surface when a family member discloses, or is dealing with aspects of sexual orientation, can be best dealt with by a competent social worker trained in family systems. Such issues must be viewed as deficits within the environment, dysfunctional transactions among environmental systems, or as a lack of individual or family coping skills or strategies (Loppnow 1985). Providing education for workers involved in prevention of placement and protection of these young people would help workers feel competent about addressing issues of sexual orientation while these youongsters are still in their own homes, and could support families and prevent out-of-home placement of many.

Family preservation programs with their primary goal of keeping families together can deliver these services within the context of the client's natural environment—their homes. Programs like the Homebuilder model (Kinney et al. 1991) have opportunities to help families with a young person who identifies or may later identify as gay or lesbian. Working with families in their natural environments makes social workers in a family preservation program ideally situated to see what is really going on in a family's home. By being in the home, the worker is able to make an accurate assessment and design an intervention that would support and preserve the family system. With a greater awareness of sexual orientation, workers in family preservation programs could educate parents as well as model and shape new behaviors. Increasing the family's knowledge about homosexual orientation (Borhek 1983, 1988; Dew 1994; Fairchild and Haywood 1989; Griffin, Wirth, and Wirth 1986; McDonald and Steinhorn 1990; Silverstein 1977; Strommen 1989), and knowing about resources such as Parents and Friends of Lesbians and Gays (PFLAG 1990), are important ways to strengthen and support the families of gay and lesbian adolescents.

Child welfare professionals who facilitate services for young gays/lesbians by providing them with accurate and relevant information about their emerging identity also play an important role in this process. Furnishing them with literature written by other gay and lesbian young people for gay and lesbian young people is one of the most beneficial techniques that can be employed (see Alyson 1991; Due 1995; Heron 1994; Kay, Estepa, and Desetta 1996; Miranda 1996; Monette 1992; Valenzuela 1996; Wadley 1996a, 1996b). Videos and guest speakers can also be used in this process. The World Wide Web or the Superinformation Highway (see http://WWW.youth.org/resources.html; http://WWW.qrd.org/qrd/youth/; http://WWW.vector.net/cariboo/youth), has been useful in liberating gays and lesbians from their extreme isolation, supplying them limitless opportunities to communicate with other gays and lesbians in chat-rooms, bulletin boards, and informational sites. Such information is useful in assisting gay- or lesbian-oriented persons in abolishing myths and stereotypes and correcting misconceptions about their identity. This information can also help educate straight teens about their gay and lesbian peers (Berkley 1996; Greene 1996).

Support groups for youths, particularly where they can find peer support, safe-space drop-in centers, as well as trained and affirming school counselors, clergy, and parents can help these young people in developing a positive self-concept and move further toward a healthy adulthood (see Robinson 1991; Soderlind 1992; Vergara 1984). Developing a positive self-concept is an essential element for healthy development.

In cases where family preservation or family support programs have not been able to preserve the family, finding appropriate out-of-home placements becomes a key task. The placement of lesbian and gay adolescents in nonsensitive foster and group homes frequently leads to placement failure, a low incidence of family reunification, and in many cases homelessness (Mallon 1994a). Making out-of-home placements safe for all young people, including gays and lesbians, should be of paramount importance to child welfare professionals. To do this, these professionals must focus their best energies on creating safe and affirming environments to help all young people grow into healthy, well-adjusted adults, including gays and lesbians.

The apparent difficulties encountered in transactions between most gay and lesbian adolescents and their family systems have inhibited many child welfare professionals from attempting to reunite these families. Although family reunification is generally not typical for the gay or lesbian adolescent who enters the out-of-home child welfare placement, reunification must not be completely rejected as an eventual permanency planning goal. Some families, after a period of cooling down following the initial shock of disclosure, are ready to work toward reunification with the child. The reflections of one child welfare professional in Los Angeles were representative of many of the professionals interviewed:

> We're all for family reunification but I think it is more difficult for gay and lesbian kids to reunite. There needs to be an openness on the part of the parents and they need sensitivity training. We try to facilitate a healthier communication between them and their teenager, but reunification can only happen after the families are educated. There also needs to be some changes in the family system. We have to help kids to readjust to being out with their families and we have to help families become knowledgeable about caring for a child who is gay or lesbian. But first all of the secrets and hiding which has happened, needs to be dealt with.

Family therapy can also facilitate reunification, but many child welfare professionals will have to learn how to work sensitively toward openly confronting sexual orientation with adolescents and families. If reunification is deemed not to be an appropriate goal, gay and lesbian adolescents should be prepared for independent living.

Additional alternatives for meeting the needs of gay and lesbian adolescents who require out-of-home placements should also be explored. Two alternatives are family foster care utilizing gay and lesbian adults as foster parents (Ricketts 1991; Ricketts and Achtenberg 1987, 1990), and group homes designed for gay and lesbian adolescents who cannot fit into existing group home programs (Mallon 1994a). Although lesbian and gay foster parenting and group home programs designed for gay/lesbian adolescents remain controversial, these alternatives have been tested. Los Angeles, New York, Toronto, Washington D.C., Philadelphia, and many other cities have used such approaches with success. These programs offer nurturing and safe environments for young people who have had difficulty finding a good fit with their own families or within existing child welfare systems.

Finally, consideration must also be given to these matters at the policy-making levels (CWLA 1991; CWA/COFCCA 1994; Taylor 1994). Professionals operating in the absence of clearly stated policies necessarily use their own personal experiences as a guide, which in the case of dealing with homosexually oriented youths can lead to conclusions based on cultural, religious, and societal biases. Written, formal policies help prevent discrimination, harassment, and verbal abuse of self-declared gays and lesbians and those perceived to be so.

An early formulation by Gil (1979) which identified three forms of institutional abuse (systemic, programmatic, and individual nonfamilial) could be useful in building institutional capacity for creating more supportive and affirming out-of-home-care environments for gay/lesbian adolescents. Systemic changes to reform the out-of-home-care system and intrafamilial education for retraining the families of gay and lesbian young people are also critical elements necessary for transforming environments.

Analogous to the child welfare delivery system deficits that have been documented for people of color communities, the problems encountered by gay and lesbian adolescents and their families are frequently ignored and largely unrecognized by the majority of child welfare professionals. An understanding of the impact of societal stigmatization of gay/lesbian individuals and their families is crucial to the recognition of, and response to, the needs of this population.

Effecting changes in professional attitudes and beliefs that could lead to creating affirming environments that can provide a good fit, and urging professionals to provide competent practice with gay and lesbian adolescents and their families, requires education, training, systemic transformation, and self-exploration on both individual and institutional levels. The development of practice competence and the creation of safe environments in this area is one positive step toward the establishment of appropriate gay- and lesbian-affirming child welfare services to address the needs of these young people and their families. Collaborations between openly gay and lesbian child welfare professionals and those who are heterosexually oriented are an essential part of this process as these services cannot be developed for gay and lesbian people, but must be developed and designed by them.

Although the issue of gay or lesbian sexual orientation is frequently framed as a "behavior" which is objectionable to some, the disclosure of one's sexual orientation is the real threat to Western society. As long as gays and lesbians in child welfare settings neither name it nor claim it, child welfare professionals can pretend that they do not exist. Once gays and lesbians begin to push their way out of the closet and begin to call attention to the injustices they have previously suffered in silence, things will begin to change. That is what this book has been about—calling attention, in the voice of those who were most affected, to the lack of fit that exists in most child welfare agencies for gay and lesbian adolescents.

As gay and lesbian young people adapted to their lives growing up in the margins of society, they struggled as well with trying to develop an internal sense of fit. Finding that they could not live with their families and then finding that they were not welcome or safe in many out-of-home-care settings, more than half of the young people sought out the relative safety of the streets as an alternative to living in care. Although the final chapter offers possible answers, some suggestions, and some models for changing these systems, it does not offer guarantees. There are no quick fixes for the problems confronting gay and lesbian adolescents within the child welfare system. There is no single policy or magic program that will erase the abuse and poor fits which most have endured. We must acknowledge the limits of our policies. The collaboration and collectivities of many people are necessary for establishing the social changes necessary for creating affirming environments for gay and lesbian adolescents. Although the issues are complex, we must believe that change is possible. As we enter the twenty-first century, the child welfare community is presented with opportunities once again, to recognize how oppression hurts and makes each of us less.

APPENDIX 1

│A Field Experience in Retrospect│

I began this study in 1991 as part of my doctoral dissertation in social welfare from the City University of New York and subsequently expanded the study to include populations of gay and lesbian young people in out-of-home child welfare placements in Los Angeles and Toronto. Largely because of my own twenty years of professional experiences in working in out-of-home child welfare in New York, and also because I am myself an openly gay man, I felt comfortable from the beginning with the prospect of working with gay and lesbian adolescents in out-of-home-care settings.

Given that there was almost no conceptualization and theory building around the phenomena of gay and lesbian adolescents in out-of-home child welfare settings, and given that the parallels between the processes of conducting grounded theory research and direct practice are multiple, the use of a grounded theory approach in the development of knowledge seemed warranted. Since the methods of such an approach are steeped in the natural world, the world of multiple variables, multiple experiences, and multiple meanings, which resonates with the world of social work practitioners (Gilgun 1994:115). "Real world problems," noted Schon (1995:34), "do not come well formed. Instead, they tend to present themselves as problematic situations, messy, and indeterminate." The process then, of doing grounded theory research with all of its untidiness, its ambiguity, and its messiness seemed so natural to me as a practitioner that it was a fit "like sliding a hand into a well-made glove" (Gilgun 1994:115).

Grounded Theory Research

The roots of the grounded theory movement are found in the work two sociologists at the University of California, Barney Glaser and Anselm

Strauss, who were studying the experiences of hospital personnel with dying patients (Glaser and Strauss 1965). Their approach was articulated more thoroughly in a subsequent text (Glaser and Strauss 1967); expanded upon and refined in other work (Glaser 1978, 1992; Strauss 1987; Strauss and Corbin 1990), and utilized by others (Charmaz 1990; Gerson 1991; Gilgun 1994; Mizrahi and Abramson 1994) who sought to promote a research process through which adequate sociological theory could be developed.

Glaser and Strauss's (1967) original work proposed a research process through which adequate sociological theory could be developed. They believed that adequate theory could emerge only from intensive involvement with the phenomenon under study. Describing "grounded theory" as a method by which theory is induced through empirical observation, this model provided the theoretical basis for my study of the experiences of gay and lesbian adolescents in North America's child welfare system.

In taking a fresh look at and working toward discovering the multiple experiences of gay and lesbian adolescents in U.S. and Canadian out-of-home-care systems, using the methodology of grounded theory enabled me to develop theories that helped me in finding ways to define concepts, to recognize relationships among concepts, and to discover patterns in the processes (Gilgun 1994:116).

While conducting this research, I was determined to remain open to the data and to approach them without my own biases, hypotheses, or preconceived notions about what I would find. As the research proceeded, I continually placed my emerging empirical findings against new data. Such data collection and data analysis involve a series of comparisons. As such, the research effort is a process of discovery and reformulation, a process of what Glaser and Strauss term "constant comparative method," a phrase which connotes the continual comparisons done within and across cases. "The concepts and the hypotheses developed," notes Gilgun (1994:116), "through these processes are inextricably linked to the empirical world, hence the name grounded theory." These links are presented clearly in the findings where the more abstract concepts and hypotheses are presented in concert with the concrete data that support them.

Theoretical Sampling

As new data were collected, I shaped further investigation by focusing on the most promising material to develop from the field. This process, for which Glaser and Strauss (1967) used the term "theoretical sampling," describes the generating of theory from data and the use of illustrative characteristics to present the theory. Theoretical sampling enabled me to be guided by the theory that emerges as the data were collected. As such, I was able to simultaneously collect, code, and analyze data.

In generating grounded theory, the initial decisions about where to begin data collections are based in a general way on the existing literature. Unlike the application of deductive methods, however, initial research decisions were not based on a preconceived theoretical framework. As an inductive process, this method of theory development relies on what the investigator learns about the experience. Theoretical propositions emerge from the data instead of the data being used to test previously generated propositions. The process began with a partial framework of logically related concepts. Then, as concepts were discovered, emerging theory developed, which pointed me toward the next steps. In some cases I did not know where these steps would lead until I identified gaps in the theory, noting disparity between observations in the field and the existing theory or by returning to the literature to examine research questions suggested by previous answers.

Although I originally intended to interview every gay or lesbian adolescent in foster homes or group homes whom I could identify, I later opted for using the strategy of theoretical saturation (Glaser and Strauss 1967: 61–62, 111–12). Theoretical saturation occurs in three ways: first, when no new or relevant data seems to emerge regarding a category; second, when the category development is dense, and all of the paradigm elements are accounted for; and finally, that the relationships between the categories are well established and validated. I knew in this study that I had reached theoretical saturation on two counts: first, when I began to repeatedly hear a version of the same story from a number of different adolescents in different agencies, in all three cities; second, when I began to meet the characters from other people's stories and began to hear the other individual's version of the same story, which confirmed the validity of the interviews and verified the information gathered from them.

In reality however, I realize that one can never reach an absolute theoretical saturation. The findings of this grounded theory study, like most others, are everlastingly open-ended. Remaining open to unanticipated insights from new evidence was a challenge. In a sense it was a task reminiscent of completing a large jigsaw puzzle, where one completes individual sections first, which will ultimately lead one to successfully completing the whole puzzle.

Data Collection Methods

Data collection methods used in this study were open-ended semistructured interviews, participant observation, and document analysis, both personal documents in the form of diaries and letters from young people and more formal documents such as social service reports and records. Open-ended interviews as the primary means for data collection allowed the respondents to describe what was meaningful and salient without being pigeonholed into standardized categories. Since this grounded theory research project used open-ended interviews, the product of this research was characterized by an emphasis on the multiple experiences and points of view of informants.

Involvement with Informants

Observation and interviewing with the fifty-four gay and lesbian young people in the study brought me into the social world of these informants. The study took place in the natural settings where young gays and lesbians in out-of-home care lived their lives. To explore the multiple experiences and to examine the strategies they used in searching for a "good fit," I taped in-depth interviews with each of the fifty-four young people and ninety-six child welfare professionals whom I interviewed over the course of a four-year period (1991–1995).

Two interview protocols (available from me by request) were employed, one for adolescents and the other for professional staff. In an effort to assess the clarity of the questions and their quality for evoking responses to the experience of the gay or lesbian adolescent in out-of-home-care settings, both protocols were pretested with five adolescents known to me and with two staff representatives. The interviewees were asked for their reactions to the questions and to the order in which they were asked, and for their suggestions for improvement and for any other questions they feel might assist the researcher at getting at the material desired. These interviews were also used to assess the value of taping. Since this research was exploratory and the emphasis on using descriptive material for conceptual development, the explicit content of these interviews are used in the final report.

Adolescent Informants

The interview guide for adolescents focused on eight major areas of inquiry, namely: descriptions of first awareness of "difference"; relationship with family; relationship with peers; initial reason for placement; description of current placement; experience with staff, both positive and negative; experience with other residents, both positive and negative; and recommendations for changes in the system. For each of these areas, preliminary questions were identified and probes were used to assist in following up with questions. The questions were designed to elicit examples, critical incidents, descriptive details, and to capture the positive and negative experiences of gay and lesbian adolescents in this setting. Young people were informed that the foci of the interviews were their reflections on their first sense of awareness of perceived "differentness"; of their relationship to their family of origin, their friendships, their experiences in the child welfare system, and their own attitudes about growing up gay or lesbian. Young people were also told that the study wanted to know their ideas about what could be done to help other gay and lesbian adolescents growing up away from their families.

In New York, where the study was launched, I placed notices in selected youth-oriented newspapers and on specially prepared flyers that were placed in both mainstream child welfare agencies and in support agencies known to be frequented by gay/lesbian young people. These announcements permitted respondents to arrange for an interview appointment calling a designated phone number, or made it known that interviews would be taking place at a particular location, giving time and date, should they want to participate. In Toronto and Los Angeles, where I had extensive contacts with professional colleagues, I visited group homes and youth programs that worked specifically with gays/lesbians in out-of-home care. To supplement these data collection approaches, those who were interviewed often identified peers and acquaintances whom they felt would be interested in the study. At the conclusion of the interview session, a participant received a small financial reimbursement. Interviews with adolescents were conducted in offices provided by cooperating agencies or in my office.

Professional Informants

The professional staff's interview guide followed a similar format but focused on issues of service delivery, namely: general knowledge about and ability to identify the population; knowledge of resources; knowledge of the needs of the population; general impressions about the gay or lesbian adolescent from various child welfare professionals; general impressions about this population from heterosexually oriented adolescents; racial, cultural, or religious issues with respect to this population; issues regarding training; identification of best placement situations for this population; and recommendations for changes. The open-ended questions were designed to elicit examples, critical incidents, descriptive details, and to capture the positive and negative experiences of gay and lesbian adolescents in this setting.

Interviews with professional staff were used to corroborate the young people's experiences. In almost every case, these professionals were corroborators in this process. Data from these interviews are woven into the fabric of this book, but their stories are not the core. These interviews focused on issues of service delivery, namely: general knowledge about and ability to identify the population; knowledge of resources; knowledge of the needs of the population; general impressions about the gay or lesbian adolescent from various child welfare professionals; racial, cultural, or religious issues with respect to this population; issues regarding training; identification of best placement situations for this population; and recommendations for changes.

In New York, where most (n=78) of the professional staff were interviewed, when I tried to arrange interviews with all fifty-nine of the voluntary child-caring agencies that contract with the City of New York and provide out-of-home care services to adolescents, all but one agency agreed to participate. Officials in the city's Child Welfare Administration (recently renamed the Administration for Children's Services—ACS) and professionals in agencies that worked exclusively with gay/lesbian youths in counseling and street out-reach programs all agreed to be interviewed.

In Los Angeles, child welfare professionals from one agency known for its group homes for gay/lesbian adolescents gave their full and complete cooperation. California public child welfare officials, as well as professionals in gay/lesbian youth-serving agencies, also participated, but more cautiously.

In Toronto, a counseling agency that has been addressing the needs of gay/lesbian youths since 1975 and a major mainstream child welfare agency were extremely open to the interview process. Professionals in street-outreach and gay/lesbian-specific programs also added invaluably to this study.

Professional staffs were contacted via telephone to schedule an interview date and time convenient for them. Interviews with professionals were conducted either in their agency offices in all three cities or in my office in New York, whichever was most convenient for the respondent. In a few cases (n=2), when it was inconvenient to schedule a face-to-face interview, or when respondents claimed that they had nothing to share in an interview because of their lack of knowledge and experience (n=10), interviews were conducted by phone.

All informants were guaranteed anonymity and total confidentiality and similar information was printed on a copy of the consent form they were given, which they were asked to sign at the time of the face-to-face interview. The protocol for assuring such confidentiality was reviewed and approved by the Institutional Review Board of the Hunter College Committee for the Protection of Human Subjects from Research Risks. In addition, the agencies assisting me in identifying subjects also reviewed and approved this protocol. The time spent in interviewing each young person and professional varied considerably, depending on that individual's schedule, but the average interview lasted two hours.

Data Analysis

In qualitative research approaches the data are almost always words, here in the form of field notes, audiotapes, and documents. Data management of 150 transcribed interviews was challenging and was done with content analysis. All interview data were obtained, recorded, entered into the computer, and coded by me, using a computer software program (Seidel, Kjolseth, and Seymour 1988), which assisted with the management of the information. Using such a system has enabled me to develop a systematic and comprehensive classification scheme to identify patterns and themes for further analysis and interpretation.

Grounded theory methods are oriented toward exploration, discovery, and inductive logic. In my analysis of the data obtained I began with specific observations and built toward general patterns, categories, and dimensions of analysis emerged from the open-ended interviews and observations. This strategy allowed important analytic dimensions to emerge from patterns found in the cases studied without presupposing in advance what the important dimensions would be.

Themes and patterns emerged from analysis of the data in two ways: as indigenous topologies and as analyst-generated topologies. The first are categories developed and articulated by the young people and professionals studied which organized the presentation of particular themes.

The second category developed as I became aware of categories or patterns for which study participants did not have specific labels or terms, and for these I have developed my own terms to describe these inductively generated categories.

Trusting that themes and patterns would emerge from the collection of data via the semistructured interviews, I searched for analogues to understand them, attempted to be conscious about a respondent's use of metaphor to describe phenomena, and searched for similarities in different patterns and concepts.

The findings are focused on understanding individual situations and testing to see whether findings in one or multiple situations can illuminate and be relevant in other situations. This process of testing to determine if previous findings are relevant to a new situation is called "pattern matching," or testing for goodness of fit which, in this study, acts as a double metaphor, for it is used in both the methodology and as a theory frame for the situation studied.

Analysis with grounded theory data that yields thick description (Geertz 1973) is a time-consuming, multidimensional, labor-intensive process that required me to live for as long as possible with complexities and ambiguities that informants presented to me, trying to come to terms with them, and ultimately, to let them go to the reader in a form that clarifies and deepens them (Miles and Huberman 1984:251). It was a process as well of resisting the temptation for premature closure, and developing an ability to live with the complexity relying on theoretical sensitivity, which indicates an awareness of the subtleties of meaning of the data.

In an attempt to remain bias-free, and to produce a valid and reliable theory, I frequently had to challenge myself periodically to step back from the data to remain objective, to maintain an attitude of skepticism, and to follow the research procedures of good science. Throughout this study, I utilized colleagues grounded in practice and theory to help reflect on the data, realizing that one who was not immersed in it could sometimes see and/or validate dimensions that I could not see. This procedure was further used as a check against my own inherent bias.

In the final analysis, because the qualitative analyst's efforts at uncovering themes, patterns, and categories are a creative process, I was required to make careful considered judgments about what was truly significant and meaningful data. Operating in the absence of statistical tests to inform me when an observation of a pattern was significant, I had to rely on my own intelligence, experience, and judgment. As this occurred,

I was aware of difference, of particularity, of that which was contradictory, and that which was paradoxical, and in doing so realizing, that which was discovered may be quantitatively insignificant, but its presence may have questioned a more conventional interpretation and thus expand understanding (Opie 1992). I was also aware throughout this process that the experiences of these fifty-four participants could not be broadly generalized to all young gays/lesbians in out-of-home child welfare settings since these informants could speak only about their own experiences. I have kept these hazards and criteria for assessing qualitative data analysis, as elaborated upon elsewhere by others (Altheide and Johnson 1994; Drisko 1997; Guba & Lincoln 1981; Reid 1994) in mind throughout these investigations and, I hope, my deliberate effort has minimized the risks.

The narratives in this book and the interpretations of them report on the experiences of young gays and lesbians as they strive for the best fit with the environments in which they live. This study depicts, in fifty-four versions, both the incongruity and the resemblance between the prevailing culture's versions of gays/lesbians who cannot or should not live at home with their families and so are placed in out-of-home care and the actually lived experiences of those in that situation. The individual nature of these young people's narratives of their lives accords us with rich opportunities to be open to the unfolding of local knowledge, on which direct practice can be and, indeed, should be built.

In exploring such inclinations, one must proceed with care. In abandoning the role of "expert" and instead entering into a collaborative search for meaning with subjects, I wished to create an openness to local knowledge, to listen to these young people's voices, to their narratives, and to their constructions of reality. In doing so, I wished to present a study grounded in the subject's experience that can speak in the voices of these young people in the margins. This strategy presents a very different kind of scenario than the large-scale epidemiological studies. This study examines the particular, pays attention to difference and, most vital, allows multiple voices to emerge to tell their own stories. As such, the questions asked and the interpretations of the data are developed in collaboration between the investigator (me) and the gay/lesbian adolescent in out-of-home care who is, after all, the expert.

This study, which was guided theoretically throughout by the work of Glaser and Strauss (1967), was also inspired by the eloquent work of

Elliot Liebow (1967, 1993) and Barbara Simon (1987). The historian Barbara Tuchman's (1979:37) advice to submit oneself to the material, instead of trying to impose oneself on the material, provided additional direction that granted me permission to step aside and allow the data to ultimately speak to and supply the answers. Guidance was additionally provided by Festinger's (1983) study, which was among the first in child welfare to permit the voices of young people to emerge from her data. In modeling my own work after the style of these scholars, I too hope to permit these young people and the child welfare professionals who deal with them, to tell their own story in their own words.

The stories and narratives of gay and lesbian adolescents in out-of-home care recorded here replace the myths associated with them with the first-person observations that are necessary components for the development of local knowledge (Geertz 1983; Hartman 1990, 1992, 1994). These young people also shed light on the twin imperatives of adolescent development and coming out that Hetrick and Martin (1987), Sullivan and Schneider (1987), and Hunter and Schaecher (1987) identified in earlier work.

Another major gift that gay and lesbian adolescents in out-of-home care offer is a first-person account of hiding one's sexual orientation from a society that presumes heterosexuality. Disempowerment strategies employed by dominant groups, as well as the technological pollution that endangers the health and well-being of individuals, impose enormous adaptive tasks on gay and lesbian young people. The effects of adapting to a hostile environment through hiding one's sexual identity are far-reaching and devastating in their impact on one's psychological state and have particular relevance to the experiences of those gay and lesbian adolescents in out-of-home care as disempowerment and social pollution are expressions of destructive relationships between the person and environments.

APPENDIX 2

|Biographies of Young Gays and Lesbians|

Note: The following young people's biographies have been greatly condensed from the original tapes. Most of the histories reflect the central theme of this book—searching for a good fit. All of the names and any identifying information has been changed to protect confidentiality. These narratives are filled with stories about families, about the experience of multiple placements, and both positive and negative experiences within the out-of-home child welfare systems. These brief biographies highlight the central themes in these young people's narratives. I have included them for the sake of completeness and to give a name to the multiple voices included in the text, and for whatever intrinsic interest and value they may have for the reader.

Albert (Toronto) is a 20-year-old Caucasian. He first realized he was gay when he was 17.

Al came into care at age 14 after his mother died and his father remarried. He comes from "a very red neck town" and was depressed after the death of his mother. His narrative about his group homes is filled with violence and abuse: "To survive you have to hide, you have to act straight." Scanning the environment for others who are "like you" and safety were important issues that he highlighted. He said: "I'm learning about gay society, gay community, gay terminology, the more I'm beginning to understand and see who is and who's not. You always got this radar out."

Alejandro (New York) is a 17-year-old Latino, who first realized he was gay at age 10.

Alejandro came into placement because of conflict with his stepmother. He claimed that he could no longer tolerate his stepmother's harassment about his being gay. He claims that he has never had sex with a same-gendered individual, yet he is certain that he is gay. He has only been in one group home and he says that his experience has been a positive one.

Alex (Toronto) is a 17-year-old Jamaican-born Canadian. He says that he has known that he is gay since he was a child.

Alex's narrative details a history of his family's verbal and physically abusive behavior toward him. He suggests that his family's culture was responsible for his maltreatment. "The Jamaican culture," he reported, "is antihomosexual; if you lived there and were gay, you'd be dead. You'd have to hide yourself especially from the older people. The religion always says that it has to be a man and a woman so most of them are wrapped up in that and they can't accept difference and it's a sin if you are different." Presently, he has no contact with his family. After several placements, a few months on the streets, and by his description, "an okay group home," Alex is satisfied with his current living arrangement. He says, "You can be more open and be your self. You don't have to hide, you can be yourself, accept yourself and be who you are. In other places, I couldn't, I had to keep to myself. Here you can express yourself more and people know what you've been through. You can learn from the role models, they are openly gay, you don't have to guess what their sexual orientation is, you know."

Angelo (Los Angeles) is a 17-year-old Mexican American. He realized he was gay at age 8.

Angelo speaks in heavily accented English, with a strong Mexican inflection in his voice. He is stocky in stature with dark features. Angelo has been in several Los Angeles agencies but was finally placed, at his lawyer's request, in a gay-affirming group home. Angelo reports that he was unmercifully teased by peers in his other group homes after gay-oriented magazines were discovered in his room. He has been in placement since he was 12 years old. Angelo sometimes dresses in opposite-gendered clothing, called cross-dressing. About this he says, "I didn't have the freedom to cross-dress in the other places. Here being gay, cross-dressing is not an issue, this place helps individuals to know who they are. Whatever the issue here, people are accepting." About his experience in the group home he says, "Places like this help people to accept others as they are. It helps you build self-esteem. It's a home away from home."

His mother is deceased, his father was unable to care for him and his three siblings, who are now cared for by an aunt who cannot accept Angelo's gay identity.

Barb (Los Angeles), an 18-year-old African American, identified herself as gay when she was 12.

Barb has short hair, wears baggy jeans and a top, and appears at first glance to be "tough." She recalled her experience in a locked facility: "In jail or juvenile hall, during an interview they ask you about your sexuality and I told them I was a lesbian. They told me not to talk the way I do. They'd say to act like a so-called woman." Her recollections about her family were associated with a strong religious bias against gay and lesbian people: "They were the worst! My grandmother took me to the preacher to ask him to pray for me so the devil wouldn't take over me. I had the church praying for me. They told me it was an abomination. The Christian part of my family had a real hard time with me being a lesbian."

Brenda (Los Angeles) is a 20-year-old African American. She came to understand her sense of being different at age 11.

Brenda has been in several placements, leaving most of them to live on the streets. She is currently living in an affirming group home in Los Angeles. Her relationship with her family is, by her own account, nonexistent: "My mom doesn't talk to me. I don't have a home anymore." Through all of her hard times, Brenda is sassy and fun. She is well-liked by her peers, and staff also reported to have enjoyed working with her.

Carl (New York), a 17-year-old Jamaican immigrant, identified as gay at age 14.

Carl remembers with great sadness how he was sent for by his mother and how she rejected him at the airport when he arrived: "She didn't even kiss me hello, she said 'hi' to everyone else and just glared at me." Carl reported that his mother knew he was gay since he was little, but she hated it. Upon his arrival to New York he lived with an aunt who accused him of trying to turn her son gay, at which point he was told by her that he would have to leave her home. He initially lived in a youth shelter, was sent to several group homes he described as "horrible," and eventually was placed in a gay-affirming group home that was accepting of his lifestyle.

Celine (Toronto) is a 19-year-old Caucasian. She identified as lesbian at age 15.

Celine has had multiple placements. Her narrative focused primarily on the aspect of hiding that was common in many young people's lives. "You have to hide, you can't come out and say what you are. You have to hide a lot of your papers and stuff." Her solution to hiding is simple in her eyes: "I think that they need to have a lot more gay counselors, gay workers, some that a gay kid could relate to."

Don (Toronto) is a 19-year-old Caucasian. He first realized he was gay when he was 12.

Don is animated and direct. His narrative suggests that staff set the tone for heterosexual young people's attitudes toward gays and lesbians in the group home. "I had this male staff bugging me about being gay and then the rest of the kids started in on me. I actually ran away from a couple of group homes because I didn't like them. I never went back to the same ones. I ended up in four different ones, I would go from one to the next."

Eddie (New York) is a 17-year-old Latino. He first identified as gay at age 12.

Eddie is tall, skinny, and very effeminate. He wears two earrings for pierced ears and very stylish clothing. His manner is affected and he uses elaborate and dramatic hand gestures. Eddie is currently placed in an affirming group home. He was previously placed in a group home he described as "a nightmare, a living hell!" "The boys there," he said, "were so rough. I just hung out with this one big kid so he could protect me and he did." He recalls "when they told me that I was coming here, I just knelt down and thanked God for hearing my prayers."

Fred (New York), an 18-year-old Latino, knew he was gay when he was 13.

Fred is HIV positive, a hemophiliac, drug-addicted, and lives on the streets. He has been in numerous out-of-home-care and juvenile justice placements. His mother, who was drug-addicted. could not care for her children and subsequently, after living with friends and relatives, mother and son were placed when Fred was seven. Fred is tall, dresses in casual street clothes, and is very articulate.

Gayle (New York) is a 19-year-old African American who first understood she was a lesbian when she was 13.

Gayle is living in a foster home where she cannot be herself and dare not tell her foster mother that she is a lesbian. She is heavy-set and "tired of hiding." She summarizes her life this way: "I couldn't be myself at home, I can be myself in this foster home, will I ever get to be who I really am?" Gayle is preparing for independent living when she can exit foster care and live her life openly as a lesbian. She heard about my study from the ad in *Foster Care Youth United* (a New York City youth newspaper) and couldn't wait to come and talk about her life.

Geoffery (Toronto) is a 17-year-old Caucasian. He realized he was gay at age 13.

Geoffery is a tall, slender, effeminate young man. He is very expressive with his hands and speaks in an affected tone. After being placed in four different foster homes and two group homes, where he was verbally and physically harassed by both peers and staff, he has finally found a good fit in an affirming program in Toronto. Geoffery entered care when his parents ejected him from their home after he came out to them.

Gerald (New York) is a 20-year-old Trinidadian. He self-identified as gay when he was 12.

Gerald dresses in punk style with a dramatic spiked, multicolored hairstyle. He wears spiked bracelets and other punk-identified jewelry. He is a formidable and threatening-looking person who has, at his own admission, adopted such a style of fashion to deter others from, as he put it, "messin' with me." Gerald has been in several congregate care placements, leaving the last to live in the streets when his friend, who also lived there, was killed by another resident because she refused to give him a cigarette. He said, "If she got killed for doing that, imagine what they would do to me if they found out that I was gay." After four months of living on the streets, he was referred by his social worker to a gay-affirming residence where he currently resides.

James (New York) is an 18-year-old African American. He realized he was gay at age 15.

James reports that he has had over eight placements: foster homes, kinship homes, group homes, and one congregate care setting. He said:

"If you were gay, you got kicked out of the foster homes, I mean you got terminated and kicked out. In one home a kid called me a fag, I got into a fight, and the staff thought I might have been gay and they warned me that they would have to terminate me if I was. It made me closeted even more."

His comments about hiding were representative of many heard during the interviews: "I closeted myself well enough so they didn't know but they made homophobic comments and stuff—stupid faggots,' 'he is so gay.' It made me think it was totally wrong; it scared me and put me back further—after all that, who would want to come out?" James is outspoken, bright, and very direct. When asked about reuniting with his family he said: "No, I do not want to go back to live with them— my mom is a total druggie. She still has hard feelings about me being gay—she didn't accept me. I said, 'That's a part of life, that's me.' "

Janet (Toronto) is an 18-year-old Latina. She indentified herself as lesbian when she was 12.

Janet is short and stocky. She has been in multiple placements and recalls, "You got to go through a lot of shit with the group home inside and out and with the staff. I got kicked out because the staff was homophobic, this one staff member, he said he was gonna stick his cock in my crotch to show me what it was like. Staff would say things like "All you need is a good fuck." I still have nightmares about it. In some places I had to hide, but they knew anyway, and they wouldn't accept it. They were totally against gays in that group home; they told me I was not allowed to talk about being a lesbian."

Jared (New York), an 18-year-old African American, identified as gay at age 12.

Prior to living in the group home where he now currently lives, Jared lived in several other group homes and on the streets. He has almost no relationship with his mother, who is alcoholic and who is also homeless. Jared recounts verbal and physical abuse in his previous group homes and says that his current residence is "all right, at least I haven't get beat up or picked on yet."

Jason (New York) is an 18-year-old African American. He realized he was gay at age 14.

Jason is well-built, attractive, and plays football for his high school.

He said, "Most people would never believe that I am gay, because I am not their stereotype of what being gay is . . . but I am." Jason came into placement when he was 14 because he was arrested for getting into a fight with a peer. Since Jason is a gender-conforming adolescent male, he rarely has had any difficulty with staff or peers about his sexuality, but he is not open with anyone on the staff about his gay identity. Jason reports, "I have gay friends and we hang out, but that's outside the group home. I keep my business to myself because if you are open in the group home, they tear you up. I've seen it happen before. I'd rather stay hidden."

Jeremey (Los Angeles), a 19-year-old Caucasian, identified as gay at age 11.

Jeremey reports that he has been in two foster homes and three group homes. He also spent some time on the street: "I lived in the street for a while; it's like family on the streets, we are like family on the streets because we share the same experience."He is currently in a gay-affirming group home: "This is a good place, no discrimination, people are able to get along, they do not allow people to come into the home and be homophobic."

José (New York) is a 17-year-old born in the Dominican Republic. He realized he was gay when he was 12.

José is stocky, well-built, and has a stylish, spiked haircut. He was placed because he and his mother had a conflictual relationship that resulted in verbal and physical abuse after she overheard his telephone conversation with his boyfriend and "found out" that he was gay. His mother initially sent him to live with relatives in the Dominican Republic in the hope that they could change him. When he returned unchanged, the mother/son relationship deteriorated to the point that she threw him out of her home. He was placed first in a private group home where he was verbally threatened and physically assaulted by other residents and subsequently placed in an affirming agency where he found the right fit.

Joyce (Toronto) is a 21-year-old Caucasian. She realized she was lesbian at age 14.

Joyce is tall, attractive, and very soft-spoken. She currently lives independently because she was recently discharged from care. She reports that "Most staff viewed my identity as an illness. I wasn't allowed to talk about my homosexuality. I feel bad about how I was treated. It wasn't fair. I basically had a miserable experience in the group homes that I lived in."

Julia (Los Angeles) is a 17-year-old African American. She realized she was lesbian at age 12.

Julia has had many placements—some were good, some were not. About them she said, "There was only one place that it was bad; they found out I was gay 'cause I was talking on the phone to my girlfriend and the staff member told my roommate to move out. She said she thought I might get into a mood and want to have sex. They asked to have me removed because they said they didn't have a license to have gay people. When they found out I was gay they treated me different. The other place knew I was gay and treated me ok." Julia also noted how "religion definitely plays a role. I'm a Muslim and they have a problem with this—it's a sin."

Katrina (Toronto) is a 21-year-old Aborigine Canadian. She identifies as lesbian at the age of 12.

Katrina is proud of her "first person" status. She has been placed in several out-of-home placements since the age of six months. She describes her experience as "a mixture of things, being in a group home and then leaving and hanging out in the streets and going back and staying there for a bit, so it was like a back-and-forth kind of thing. When the decision was made to move me then I would go to the next place but I was always running away, going back, and then running away again. . . . It was hard in some ways because if I said I was a lesbian, it was always denied. If I said "I'm a lesbian," they said, "Oh, no you're not," it was hard. Actually, they either denied it or never said anything. Katrina is of medium build, with dark straight hair. She is extraordinarily bright and quick-witted and a great storyteller.

Kevin (New York) is a 20-year-old Caucasian. He realized his "difference" when he was 5 years old.

Kevin is short in stature, of Irish ancestry, and very hyperactive, as evidenced by the fact that he could not sit still in his chair throughout the interview. He recalls that his mother could not care for him and his siblings and consequently they were placed in a series of foster homes. He estimates that he was in about nine different foster homes. "Some were good, some were bad." He says, however, that he would never go back to them—he is now living on his own. "They treated gay kids there really bad. They didn't know about me, because I'm not very effeminate, but I saw what they did to the other gay kids who couldn't hide."

Laurence (New York) is a 21-year-old Caucasian who realized he was gay when he was about 4 or 5 years old.

Tall and handsome, Laurence works as an air conditioner repair man and lives with a roommate in an apartment in Manhattan. He was in foster care since age 9. He was placed when his mother became psychiatrically hospitalized. Laurence had both positive and negative experiences in the many foster homes and group homes he lived in. Although he spoke about the negative treatment that he witnessed gay and lesbian kids receiving in group homes, he himself never experienced such treatment, he said, because "no one ever knew that I was gay. I mean I did my stuff and all, but it was very hush-hush and no one would have ever suspected that I was gay. I played basketball, I dated girls, but . . . I was definitely gay. I just never told anyone. When I left care, I could live my life as I wanted to."

Maria (Los Angeles) is a 20-year-old Latina, born in Mexico. She realized she was a lesbian when she was about 17.

Maria is about 5'2" with long brown hair and copper-colored skin. She entered care when she was 10 and lived in a series of foster homes, pre-adoptive homes, and ultimately in several group homes. She came "into the life" as she puts it, when she was 17. Maria has a wonderful philosophy of life, "People need to be themselves, just forget what other people say; people are always gonna have something to say whether you're gay or straight, but if you be yourself—you'll be okay." She currently lives on her own. Her parents are deceased.

Maura (New York) is an 18-year-old Caucasian who identified as lesbian at age 13.

When asked how she identified, Maura said, "I prefer to be called a dyke." She was psychiatrically hospitalized after a bout with depression and a suicide attempt which she now attributes to an increasing isolation because of her emerging lesbian identity. After several unsuccessful placements in inhospitable environments that resulted in her running away from the facilities, Maura is currently placed in a group home in New York City where she feels accepted, though not wholly understood, by most staff and peers. Maura is bright, verbal, short in stature, and sports an equally short haircut.

Maurice (New York) is a 21-year-old Caucasian. He realized he was gay when he was 8 years old.

Maurice is tall, slender, and very hyperactive. He is effeminate and very open about his sexuality to the point of being flirtatious with almost everyone he comes in contact with. Maurice spent seven years in foster care. He came into care because he and his mother could not get along and she could no longer tolerate his late hours. Maurice claims to have been in five different groups. He said, "One was worse than the next. I mean they were horrible, they had these terrible boys there and the staff . . . they were worse than the kids . . . so homophobic, so unprofessional. . . . I was so glad to get out of there, the last group home wasn't so bad that was because they had gay staff there and they watched my back."

Michelle (Los Angeles) is a 17-year-old Caucasian. She reallized she was lesbian at age 13.

Michelle reports that she has been in fourteen other agencies. "I've been in placement since I was four." Michelle is tall, slender, and very attractive. She reports that after living on the streets ("I got here because I didn't want to live on the streets") it's been cool—it's nice. I feel comfortable. I can open up and act the way I always wanted to act here."

Miguel (New York), a 19-year-old Latino, realized he was different when he was 8.

Miguel hitchhiked from Nicaragua to Miami when he found it impossible to continue to live there after he came out to his extended family. His story is filled with details about his journey from Nicaragua to first Miami and later to New York City. To support himself while on his journey, Miguel prostituted himself. Finding New York City to be more difficult than he thought, he first went to a shelter and then sought to be placed in an out-of-home-care placement. His first placement was a gay-affirming one.

Mike (New York) is a 19-year-old Latino. He identified as gay at age 10.

Mike attends a gay-affirming high school and is placed in a group home. He has been in three different group homes. He was initially placed as an 8-year-old child because his parents divorced and his Dad could no longer care for him after he remarried. Mike said: "I know that I am gay, but I have never had sex with a man. I am waiting for the right one. People sometimes ask if I have never had sex with a man, then how could I know? For me, it's an internal thing—I feel it inside." Mike was closeted in his group home because, he reported, " "You have to be careful about who knows, if they know they'll treat you differently—I've seen it happen to kids before."

Patrick (Los Angeles) is a 17-year-old Caucasian. He said that he knew he was "different" at age 4.

Patrick is in his first placement at a group home in Los Angeles. Although he has had a positive experience in his group home—"I feel very liberated, I could come out. This place gives me a lot of structure and motivation to move," he describes a less-than-satisfactory experience with his family: "My brothers didn't like that I was gay—one of my brothers wouldn't let me touch his kids but they have come around. It's not fun, my parents didn't care." School was even worse, "I used to get gay bashed in school, I had people give me death threats—I get in fights a lot. People tried to have sex with me—others, football players, they would say "Would you try it with me, and I did. It was a nightmare."

Paula (Toronto) is a 20-year-old Caucasian. She realized her lesbian identity at age 10.

Paula has been in multiple placements and has lived in group homes, foster homes, and shelters. She came into placement because she had problems getting along with her mother. Reflecting on her experiences in group homes she said, "Sometimes things that go on in group homes are not that blatant, but some things are really blatant, sometimes people just refuse to talk to you. People in the system don't know how to deal with it. . . . when counselors get turned out of universities they run into things that they don't know how to deal with. And it just so happens that working with gay kids is one of those things. But nobody teaches you . . . there's some information out there but it's not like a university course. They don't know how to counsel Gay Students 101."

Peter, age 18, and and his brother **John**, age 17 (Los Angeles), are African Americans. They realized they were gay at ages 12 and 10.

Peter and John are each tall and wiry, with short hair. After their mother abandoned them, they were grudgingly taken in to live with their aunt, who is described by the brothers as being "very religious." Their aunt threw them out of her home when she "found out" that they were gay after she had read letters they written to them by same-gendered friends. Peter and John lived in the streets in L.A. for several months before entering the child welfare system. John recalls knowing he was gay this humorous way "I knew that I was gay when I saw Bruce Willis and I thought, oh, my! That's when I knew."

Philip (Toronto) is a 17-year-old African American. He realized his gay identity at age 8.

Philip has been in eleven group homes since he was 14. In most, he says, "I had to act like Mr. Straight, I had to totally act straight. In one foster home I was in the foster father always warned me to watch out for those kids in school that acted gay. Little did he know that I was one of them, but I just played along." Philip's warning to other gay and lesbian youth in care: "I don't know, I'd just say be careful who you tell—you always have to watch your back."

Ralph (New York) is a 21-year-old Caucasian. He realized he was gay at age 12.

Ralph is HIV positive and lives on the streets. He recounted a long history of being in placement. When asked how many placements he had been in he replied " I've been in too many to remember . . . I don't know—about 38, I guess." He was placed as a young child and has had limited contact with his family. "Being gay in the group home was like the worst thing you could be . . . the names, the teasing, the fighting, it was endless." After being raped by a male staff member, Ralph decided that he had "had enough" and he left care to live on the street. Ralph says emphatically, "I would never go back, life in the streets is better than that place."

Raul (Los Angeles) is an 18-year-old Latino. He identified as gay at age 13.

Raul looks older than 18, perhaps because of his black-rimmed glasses. He has been in several placements, where he recounted horrific abuse from both peers and staff. He remarked, "Being gay in a group home is terrible. You're always treated differently. The verbal abuse was constant and then sometimes it escalated into physical violence." Raul is a large, big-boned young man with a very serious demeanor. He claims that his physical size actually helped to protect him from more serious abuse.

Raymond (Los Angeles) is a 19-year-old African American. He self-identified as gay at age 15.

Raymond has lived in three different group homes. He entered care after he and his mother had a conflict about his late hours and his friends. His mother read some letters that he had in his room from a boy he was dating. When she confronted him about being gay he did not deny it and their relationship deteriorated because as he says, "A silence invaded our house. We never talked about things anymore, she just didn't want to hear it. I finally couldn't stand it anymore and I left—that's when I came into care—it was worse!"

Remee (Los Angeles) is an 18-year-old African American. She said she "always knew" she was lesbian.

Remee has had eight different placements in a variety of settings: group homes, foster homes, and locked facilities. She reports: "I came into care because I got tired of hiding. My foster home, they didn't want me to be around the kids—I mean they were two years old, who'd want them. They thought that I was going to do something to them. It was a family group home—I guess they thought I'd hurt a 288 one of them [child molestation]." Remee is a very serious young woman who, after many placements, is now in an affirming placement in Los Angeles. She says: "This is the best place to be if you have to be in a group home because you can be yourself."

Richard (Los Angeles) is a 17-year-old African American. He realized he was gay at age 12.

Richard is tall and overweight. He has a joking manner and flirts outrageously throughout the interview. He was in several placements before coming to this group home. "I got to come here because I'm gay." He said, "I got interviewed and they accepted me—people in other places weren't comfortable with differences. My social worker was a lesbian and she referred me here."

Richard's family had a hard time accepting him: "My mother's boyfriend was abusive toward me. My grandmother couldn't deal with me either. You know those church people have a really hard time with gay people, even their own family. 'Oh Jesus, oh, glory'—the regular old religious family. . . . They make me crazy. If they are so into God and God is love and all then we should treat each other better. They say that God don't make no mistake. It was no mistake to make me a gay black man."

Robbie (New York) is a 17-year-old Latino. He realized he was gay at age 10.

Robbie is effeminate and very dramatic in his appearance and manner. He tells of graphic verbal and physical abuse by his mother and equally unpleasant experiences in the numerous New York City-based group homes he lived in. "I could never be myself in those places and the staff there were so unprofessional. . . I mean they just hated me, some of them even told me that, others were more subtle about it, but I knew."

Sharice (New York) is a 19-year-old African American. She realized she was lesbian at age 12.

Sharice is bright, attractive, and dresses with a flair. There is an instant recognition of self-confidence about her and she commands instant respect from everyone she encounters. After being in "too many group homes to remember" and after a staff member in one of them raped her, Sharice left care and refused to return.

Sharte (New York), a 17-year-old African American, realized he was gay at age 14.

Sharte recalls his experiences in the group homes with very colorful street language: "Honey, I didn't let anyone mess with me. They tried that shit with me, but I didn't let no one get over on me. Oh, no, there were not gonna go there with me!" Sharte reports that his mother always knew, "She told me, 'Sharte, you is a faggot!' At first I felt hurt, but I knew that she was right." Sharte feels that his ability to "talk my way out of most things" was what kept him relatively safe in the many group homes that he lived in.

Shawn (New York) is an 18-year-old African American. He came to understand that he was gay when he was 8.

Shawn is stocky, well-dressed, and has been in child care for the past six years. He has had some positive and some negative experiences. He is not open in his current group home but said, "It's a pretty okay place. I mean the staff are not really well informed about gay people, but it's not a dangerous place." Shawn attends a gay-affirming high school and receives a great deal of support from the other students and teachers there.

Steven (New York) is a 17-year-old Caucasian. He said he first realized he was "different" when he was about 4 or 5 years old.

Steven left his home when his mother told him that she was afraid that he might hurt his young brothers because he was "that way." When residents in his group home found a gay magazine, they ransacked his room and physically threatened him. Steven said "It was terrible, I just couldn't take it anymore. I awoled from the program and I only came back when my social worker swore to me that she had a different placement for me." Steven reported that "things were better in the new place."

Tamil (New York), an 18-year-old African American, realized he was gay at age 10.

Tamil has been in a group home placement in New York City for three years. He was placed because his grandmother, with whom he lived, could not "deal with" his gay life. This is his first placement. He is tall, of slender build, and is a very flashy dresser who frequently experiments with innovative hair designs. His appearance, together with his assertive character, suggests to newcomers that he is very confident about himself. He is, as he notes, "quick to throw shade" (to verbally defend oneself) and extremely outspoken about the rights of gay youths. He is frequently seen by other young people as their spokesperson.

Tina (Toronto) is a 20-year-old Trinidadian. She realized she was lesbian at age 15.

Tina has been in several group home placements in Toronto. She is extremely bright, articulate, and able to point out both the positive and negative elements of her experience as a young woman in an out-of-home child welfare placement. She also reflects about the need to hide: "I think there's lots of gay and lesbian kids in care, but they hide, they hide for the same reasons I did. They may not be out but they are there. When we do come out, it's difficult, because when we do we are treated like we have a psychiatric problem. It is the discrimination that we face that effects us, most just being gay, lesbian, bisexual."

Although she did not come out in her group home, she came out as soon as she left care. Tina reflects on the negative associations that her culture had toward gay and lesbian persons: "I have no family network for support. I am Trinidadian and it was very very taboo, very antilesbian or gay. There was no connection and no networking from my family. We can't go to our community that way." Tina also astutely reports on the multiple oppressions that she has experienced: "It's definitely really, really, difficult, as a lesbian woman of color. I have so many of these difficulties—the same racism that is there in general society is there in gay communities. It multiplies the oppression I feel, it doubles it—if it's not one it's the other. The only way we become visible is to accept ourselves openly and then become visible." Tina is currently living on her own, attending college, and employed full time.

Tony (Los Angeles) is an 18-year-old African American. He self-identified as gay at age 15.

Tony is small and wiry-framed. He has had multiple placements—he can't remember how many. He was placed at the group home where he currently lives but left after three months: "I went to Santa Monica Boulevard and became a drag queen, but then I realized that I didn't want to live like that and I came back." "My parents," he said, "were terrible, they didn't understand at all—one part of me hates them and the other accepts them as they are."

Tracey (New York) is an 18-year-old light-skinned African American. He realized he was gay at age 11.

Tracey was placed by his aunt after he developed behavior problems in school, which he now identifies as reaction to his emerging gay identity. He has been in three group homes, has lived on the streets, in subway tunnels, and in one congregate care facility in upstate New York. Tracey's story is filled with verbal and physical abuse and sadness. His quote, "I mean we don't exactly get the Welcome Wagon when we come to a group home," provides the title for this book.

Treg (New York) is an 18-year-old African American. He first was aware of seeming different in junior high.

Treg is effeminate, short, and jauntily dressed in Gap clothing. He gives the impression of competence and mental alertness. Treg came into placement after a continued conflict with his mother, not having to do directly with his sexual orientation. His first placement was in a gay-affirming group home, and he notes that his experiences there with respect to his sexual orientation have been positive.

Trevor (New York) is an 18-year-old African American. He realized he was gay at age 13.

Trevor is very interested in music and is very intelligent. He came into care when he had an argument with his mother that resulted in both of them getting arrested. Trevor's mother was so angry at him when she was released after spending a weekend in jail, that she threw him out of her house. After a few weeks of living with an uncle Trevor went to the local child welfare agency to request placement. He was placed initially in a city-run group home, which he describes as "horrible," and later transferred to an affirming program, which he reports as being "better, but not great."

Wilem (Los Angeles), a 19-year-old Latino, realized he was gay at age 8.

This is Wilem's first placement, he has never lived on the street, and feels lucky that he has been placed in this affirming group home in Los Angeles. He was placed because "My parents couldn't deal with my sexuality. They'd say 'ok you are . . . . but let's not talk about it, let's leave it where it is.' They just went into shock, saying it was a phase, what did we do wrong—the usual thing. I tried to talk about it with them but they didn't want to talk about it and if they couldn't deal with that then they couldn't deal with me and I left my home."

After leaving home, he claimed, "I moved in with a friend and my parents harassed me to come back and I tried to kill myself because I didn't want to deal with it. My social worker refer me to the Gompher's Residence which has been okay for me"

Wilma (Toronto) is a 20-year-old African American who identified herself as lesbian at age 11.

Wilma lives on the streets. Her fit within the context of her family system was so poor that she left there to live in a group home. After being in five different group homes and being raped in the last by a male staff member, she escaped the "safety" of the group home to live on the streets. She maintains "It's better on the streets—at least you know who your friends are."

References

Aldgate, J., A. N. Maluccio, and C. Reeves. 1989. *Adolescents in Foster Homes.* London: B. T. Batsford; Chicago: Lyceum Books.

Altheide, D and J. Johnson. 1994. Criteria for assessing the interpretive validity in qualitative research. In N. Denzin and Y. Lincoln, eds., *Handbook of Qualitative Research*, pp. 485–499. Thousand Oaks, Calif.: Sage Publications.

Alyson, S. 1991. *Young, Gay, and Proud.* Boston: Alyson Publications.

American Psychiatric Association. 1974. *Diagnostic and Statistical Manual of Mental Disorders*, 2d ed. Washington, D.C.: American Psychiatric Association.

Annin, B. J. 1990. Training for HIV infection: Prevention in child welfare services. In G. R. Anderson, ed., *Courage to Care: Responding to the Crisis of Children with AIDS*, pp. 171–185. Washington, D.C.: Child Welfare League of America.

Athey, J. L. 1991. HIV infection and homelessness. *Child Welfare* 70(5): 517–528.

Bell, A., M. Weinberg, and S. Hammersmith. 1981. *Sexual Preference: Its Development in Men and Women.* Bloomington: Indiana University Press.

Berger, R. 1990. Passing: Impact on the quality of same-sex couple relationships. *Social Work* 35(4): 328–332.

Berkley, S. 1996. Homophobia in the group home: Overcoming my fear of gays. *Foster Care Youth United* (January/February): 17–19.

Berzon, B. 1992. Telling your family you're gay. In B. Berzon, ed., *Positively Gay: New Approaches to Gay and Lesbian Life*, pp. 67–78. Berkeley, Calif.: Celestial Arts.

Besharov, D. J., ed. 1988. *Protecting Children from Abuse and Neglect: Policy and Practice.* Springfield, Ill.: Charles C. Thomas.

Billingsley, A. and J. M. Giovannoni. 1972. *Children of the Storm.* New York: Harcourt Brace Jovanovich.

Blos, P. 1981. *The Adolescent Passage: Developmental Issues.* New York: International Universities Press.

Blumenfeld, W. J.and D. Raymond. 1993. *Looking at Gay and Lesbian Life.* Boston: Beacon Press.

Borhek, M. V. 1983. *Coming Out to Parents.* New York: Pilgrim Press.

Borhek, M. V. 1988. Helping gay and lesbian adolescents and their families: A mother's perspective. *Journal of Adolescent Health Care*, 9(2): 123–128.

Boyd-Franklin, N. 1989. *Black Families: A Multisystems Approach to Family Therapy*. New York: Guilford Press.

Brown, L. 1988. Lesbians, gay men, and their families: Common clinical issues. *Journal of Gay and Lesbian Psychotherapy* 1(1): 65–77.

Brown, P. 1991. Passing: Differences in our public and private self. *Journal of Multicultural Social Work* 1(2): 33–50.

Browning, C. 1987. Therapeutic issues and intervention strategies with young adult lesbian clients: A developmental approach. *The Journal of Homosexuality* 13(4): 45–53.

Bucy, J. and T. Able-Peterson. 1993. *The Street Outreach Training Manual*. Washington, D.C.: U.S. Dept. of Health and Human Services.

Cantwell. M. A. 1996. *Homosexuality: The Secret a Child Dare Not Tell*. San Rafael, Calif.: Rafael Press.

Cass, V. C. 1979. Homosexual identity formation: A theoretical model. *Journal of Homosexuality* 4: 219–235.

Cass, V. C. 1984. Homosexual identity formation: Testing a theoretical model. *Journal of Sex Research* 20: 143–167.

Cates, J. A. 1987. Adolescent sexuality: Gay and lesbian issues. *Child Welfare League of America* 66: 353–363.

CASMT (Children's Aid Society of Metropolitan Toronto). 1995a. *1995 Service Statistics*. [W W W document]. URL   *http://www.casmt.on.ca:80/stats.html*

CASMT. 1995b. *We Are Your Children Too: Accessible Child Welfare Services for Lesbian, Gay, and Bisexual Youth*. Toronto: Children's Aid Society of Metropolitan Toronto.

CDF (Children's Defense Fund). 1995. *State of America's Children*. Washington, D.C.: CDF.

Charmaz, K. 1990. Discovering chronic illness: Using grounded theory. *Social Science and Medicine* 30(11): 1161–1172.

Child Welfare Administration, *see* CWA.

Child Welfare League of America, *see* CWLA.

Coleman, E. 1981. Developmental stages of the coming out process. *The Journal of Homosexuality* 7(2/3): 31–43.

Coleman, M. 1986. Nontraditional boys: A minority in need of reassessment. *Child Welfare* 65(3): 252–259.

Comstock, G. D. 1991. *Violence Against Lesbians and Gay Men*. New York: Columbia University Press.

Constantine, L. and F. M. Martinson, eds. 1981. *Children and Sex*. Boston: Little, Brown.

Cook, R. 1988. Trends and needs in programming for independent living. In E. V.

Mech, *Independent-Living Services for At-Risk Adolescents*, pp. 1–18. Washington, D.C.: Child Welfare League of America.

CWA (Child Welfare Administration and Council of Family and Child Caring Agencies), eds. 1994. *Improving Services to Gay and Lesbian Youth in New York City's Child Welfare System*. New York: CWA.

CWLA (Child Welfare League of America). 1981. *Standards for Out-of-Home Care*. Washington, D.C.: CWLA.

CWLA. 1991. *Serving the Needs of Gay and Lesbian Youths: The Role of Child Welfare Agencies: Recommendations of a Colloquium, January 25–26, 1991*. Washington, D.C.: CWLA.

D'Augelli, A. R. and S. L. Hershberger. 1993. Lesbian, gay, and bisexual youth in community settings: Personal challenges and mental health problems. *American Journal of Community Psychology* 21(4): 421–448.

De Crescenzo, T. 1985. Homophobia: A study of attitudes of mental health professionals towards homosexuality. In R. Schoenberg, R. Goldberg, and D. Shore, eds., *With Compassion Towards Some: Homosexuality and Social Work in America*, pp. 115–136. New York: Harrington Park Press.

Delany, S. L., A. E. Delany, and A. H. Hearth. 1993. *Having Our Say: The Delany Sisters' First 100 Years*. New York: Dell.

De Monteflores, C. and S. J. Schultz. 1978. Coming out: Similarities and differences for lesbians and gay men. *Journal of Social Issues* 34(3): 59–72.

De Vine, J. L. 1984. A systematic inspection of affectional preference orientation and the family of origin. *Journal of Social Work and Human Sexuality* 2: 9–17.

Devore, E. and E. G. Schlesinger. 1987. *Ethnic-Sensitive Social Work Practice*. 2d ed. Columbus, Ohio: Merrill.

Dew, R. F. 1994. *The Family Heart: A Memoir of When Our Son Came Out*. Reading, Mass.: Addison-Wesley.

de Young, M. 1982. *The Sexual Victimization of Children*. Jefferson, N.C.: McFarland.

Diamond, M. 1979. Sexual identity and sexual roles. In V. Bullough, ed., *The Frontiers of Sex Research*, pp. 234–241. New York: Prometheus Books.

Diepold, J. and R. D. Young. 1979. Empirical studies of adolescent sexual behavior: A critical review. *Adolescence* 14: 45–64.

Drisko, J. W. 1997. Strengthening qualitative studies and reports: Standards to promote academic integrity. *Journal of Social Work Education* 33(1): 185–197.

Due, L. 1995. *Joining the Tribe: Growing Up Gay and Lesbian in the 90's*. New York: Anchor Books.

Erikson, E. 1950. *Childhood and Society*. New York: W. W. Norton.

Fanshel, D. 1982. *On the Road to Permanency: An Expanded Data Base for Children in Foster Care*. New York: Child Welfare League of America.

Fanshel, D. and E. Shinn. 1978. *Children in Foster Care: A Longitudinal Investigation.* New York: Columbia University Press.

Fairchild, B. and N. Hayward. 1989. *Now That You Know: What Every Parent Should Know About Homosexuality.* New York: Harcourt Brace Jovanovich.

Festinger, T. 1983. *No One Ever Asked Us: A Postscript to Foster Care.* New York: Columbia University Press.

Finnegan, D. G. and E. B. McNally. 1987. *Dual Identities: Counseling Chemically Dependent Gay Men and Lesbians.* Center City, Minn.: Hazelden Foundation.

Fitzgerald, M. D. 1996. Homeless youths and the child welfare system: Implications for policy and service. *Child Welfare* 75(3): 717–730.

Fraser, M., P. Pecora, and D. Haapala. 1991. *Families in Crisis.* New York: Aldine de Gruyter.

Garnets, L., G. M. Herek, and B. Levy. 1992. Violence and victimization of lesbians and gay men: Mental health consequences. In G. M. Herek and K. T. Berrill, eds., *Hate Crimes,* pp. 207–226. Newbury Park, Calif.: Sage Publications.

Geertz, C. 1973. *The Interpretation of Culture.* New York: Basic Books.

Geertz, C. 1983. *Local Knowledge: Further Essays in Interpretive Anthropology.* New York: Basic Books.

Germain, C. B. 1981. The ecological approach to people-environment transactions. *Social Casework: The Journal of Contemporary Social Work* 62: 323–331.

Germain, C. B. 1985. The place of community work within an ecological approach to social work practice. In S. H. Taylor and R. W. Roberts, eds., *Theory and Practice of Community Social Work,* pp. 30–55. New York: Columbia University Press.

Germain, C. B. 1991. *Human Behavior and the Social Environment.* New York: Columbia University Press.

Germain, C. B. and A. Gitterman. 1980. *The Life Model of Social Work Practice.* New York: Columbia University Press

Germain, C. B. and A. Gitterman. 1996. *The Life Model of Social Work Practice.* 2d ed. New York: Columbia University Press.

Gerson, E. M. 1991. Supplementing grounded theory. In D. R. Maines, ed., *Social Organization and Social Process: Essays in Honor of Anselm Strauss,* pp. 285–301. New York: Aldine de Gruyter.

Gil, E. 1979. *Handbook for Understanding and Preventing Abuse and Neglect of Children in Out-of-Home Care.* San Francisco: San Francisco Child Abuse Council and the San Francisco Department of Social Services.

Gilgun, J. 1994. Hand into glove: The grounded theory approach and social work practice research. In E. Sherman and W. Reid, eds., *Qualitative research in Social Work,* pp. 115–125. New York: Columbia University Press.

Glaser, B. G. 1978. *Theoretical Sensitivity.* Mill Valley, Calif.: Sociological Press.

Glaser, B. G. 1992. *Basics of Grounded Theory Analysis.* Mill Valley, Calif.: Sociological Press.

Glaser, B. G. and A. L. Strauss. 1965. *Awareness of Dying*. Hawthorne, N.Y.: Aldine.

Glaser, B. G. and A. L. Strauss. 1967. *The Discovery of Grounded Theory: Strategies for Qualitative Research*. Chicago: Aldine.

Gochros, H. L. 1985. Teaching social workers to meet the needs of the homosexually oriented. In R. Schoenberg, R. Goldberg, and D. Shore, eds., *With Compassion Towards Some: Homosexuality and Social Work in America*, pp. 137–156. New York: Harrington Park Press.

Gochros, H. L. 1995. Sex, AIDS, social work, and me. *Reflections* 1(2): 37–43.

Goffman, E. 1963. *Stigma: Notes of the Management of a Spoiled Identity*. Englewood Cliffs, N.J.: Prentice-Hall.

Gonsiorek, J. C. 1988. Mental health issues of gay and lesbian adolescents. *Journal of Adolescent Health Care* 9(2): 114–122.

Gramick, J. 1983. Homophobia: A new challenge. *Social Work* 28(2): 137–141.

Gramick, J. 1984. Developing a lesbian identity. In T. Darty and S. Potter, eds., *Women Identified Women*, pp. 31–44. Palo Alto, Calif.: Mayfield.

Greeley, G. 1994. Service organizations for gay and lesbian youth. In T. De Crescenzo, ed., *Helping Gay and Lesbian Youth: New Policies, New Programs, New Practices*, pp. 111–130. New York: Haworth Press.

Greene, B. 1990. Sturdy bridges: The role of African-American mothers in the socialization of African American children. *Women and Therapy* 10: 205–225.

Greene, Z. 1996. Straight, but not narrow-minded. In P. Kay, A. Estepa, and A. Desetta, eds., *Out With It: Gay and Straight Teens Write About Homosexuality*, pp. 12–14. New York: Youth Communications.

Griffin, C., M. J. Wirth, and A. G. Wirth. 1986. *Beyond Acceptance*. Englewood Cliffs, N.J.: Prentice-Hall.

Groth, A. N. 1978. Patterns of sexual assault against children and adolescents. In A. W. Burgess, A. N. Groth, L. L. Holmstrom, and S. M. Sgroi, eds., *Sexual Assault of Children and Adolescents*, pp. 3–24. Lexington, Mass.: Lexington Books.

Groth, A. N. and H. J. Birnbaum. 1978. Adult sexual orientation and attraction to underage persons. *Archives of Sexual Behavior* 7(3): 175–181.

Gruson, L. 1993. Meeting gay bias face to face in class: Teen-agers get direct answers. *New York Times*, October 15, p. B1.

Guba, E. and Y. Lincoln. 1981. *Effective Evaluation*. San Francisco: Jossey-Bass.

Hartman, A. 1990. Many ways of knowing [editorial]. *Social Work* 35(1): 3–4.

Hartman, A. 1992. In search of subjugated knowledge [editorial]. *Social Work* 37(6): 483–484.

Hartman, A. 1993. Out of the closet: Revolution and backlash [editorial]. *Social Work* 38(3): 245–245, 360.

Hartman, A. 1994. Setting the theme: Many ways of knowing. In E. Sherman and

W. Reid, eds., *Qualitative Research in Social Work*, pp. 459–463. New York: Columbia University Press.

Hartman, A. and J. Laird. 1983. *Family-Centered Social Work Practice*. New York: Free Press.

Hartman, A. and J. Laird. 1987. Family practice. In A. Minahan, ed., *Encyclopedia of Social Work*. 18th ed. Vol. 1, pp. 575–589. Silver Spring, Md.: National Association of Social Workers.

Hartmann, H. 1958. *Ego Psychology and the Problem of Adaptation*. New York: International Universities Press.

Herdt, G. and A. Boxer. 1993. *Children of Horizons: How Gay and Lesbian Teens Are Leading a New Way Out of the Closet*. Boston: Beacon Press.

Herek, G. M. 1990. The context of anti-gay violence: Notes on cultural psychological heterosexism. *Journal of Interpersonal Violence* 5(3): 316–333.

Herek, G. M. and K. T. Berrill, eds. 1992. *Hate Crimes: Confronting Violence Against Lesbians and Gay Men*. Newbury Park, Calif.: Sage Publications.

Hetrick, E. and A. D. Martin. 1987. Developmental issues and their resolution for gay and lesbian adolescents. *Journal of Homosexuality* 13(4): 25–43.

Holdway, D. M. and J. Ray. 1992. Attitudes of street kids toward foster care. *Child and Adolescent Social Work* 9(4): 307–317.

Hooker, E. 1957. The adjustment of the male overt homosexual. *Journal of Projective Techniques* 21: 18–31.

Hooker, E. 1967. The homosexual community. In J. Gagnon and W. Simon, eds., *Sexual Deviance*, pp. 380–392. New York: Harper and Row.

HRC (Human Rights Campaign)

Hudson, W. and W. A. Ricketts. 1980. A strategy for measurement of homophobia. *Journal of Homosexuality* 5: 357–371.

Hunter, J. 1990. Violence against lesbian and gay male youths. *Journal of Interpersonal Violence* 5(3): 295–300.

Hunter, J. and R. Schaecher. 1987. Stresses on lesbian and gay adolescents in schools. *Social Work in Education* 9(3): 180—188.

Hunter, J. and R. Schaecher. 1990. Lesbian and gay youth. In M. J. Rotherram-Borus, J. Bradley, and N. Obolensky, eds., *Planning to Live: Evaluating and Treating Suicidal Teens in Community Settings*, pp. 297–316. Tulsa: University of Oklahoma Press.

Hunter, J. and R. Schaecher. 1994. AIDS prevention for lesbian, gay, and bisexual adolescents. *Families and Society* 75(6): 93–99.

Jackson, S. 1982. *Childhood and Sexuality*. London: Basil Blackwell.

Janus, M. D., F. X. Archambault, and S. M. Brown. 1995. Physical abuse in Canadian runaway adolescents. *Child Abuse and Neglect* 19: 433–447.

Jones, C. 1978. *Understanding Gay Relatives and Friends*. New York: Seabury Press.

Kamerman, S. B. and A. J. Kahn. 1989. *Social Services for Children, Youth, and*

Families in the United States. Special Issue of *Children and Youth Services Review* 12: 1–184.

Kay, P., A. Estepa, and A. Desetta, eds. 1996. *Out With It: Gay and Straight Teens Write About Homosexuality.* New York: Youth Communications.

Kinney, J. M., D. A. Haapala, C. Booth, and S. Leavitt. 1991. *The Homebuilder's Model: Keeping Families Together.* Hawthorne, N.Y.: Aldine de Gruyter.

Kinsey, A. C., W. B. Pomeroy, and C. E. Martin. 1948. *Sexual Behavior in the Human Male.* Philadelphia: W. B. Saunders.

Kinsey, A. C., W. B. Pomeroy, C. E. Martin, and P. H. Beghard. 1953. *Sexual Behavior in the Human Female.* Philadelphia: W. B. Saunders.

Kournay, R. F. 1987. Suicide among homosexual adolescents. *Journal of Homosexuality* 13(4): 111–117.

Kruks, G. 1991. Gay and lesbian homeless/street youth: Special issues and concerns. *Journal Adolescent Health* 12(7): 515–518

Laird, J. 1979. An ecological approach to child welfare: Issues of family identity and continuity. In C. B. Germain, ed., *Social Work Practice: And Environments,* pp. 174–209. New York: Columbia University Press.

Laird, J. and A. Hartman, eds. 1985. *A Handbook of Child Welfare: Context, Knowledge, and Practice.* New York: Free Press.

Liebow, E. 1967. *Tally's Corner.* Boston: Little, Brown.

Liebow, E. 1993. *Tell Them Who I Am.* New York: Penguin.

Lindsey, D. 1994. *The Welfare of Children.* New York: Oxford University Press.

Loppnow, D. M. 1985. Adolescents on their own. In J. Laird and A. Hartman, eds., *A Handbook of Child Welfare: Context, Knowledge, and Practice,* pp. 514–532. New York: Free Press.

Lum, D. 1986. *Social Work Practice with People of Color: A Process-Stage Approach.* Monterey, Calif.: Brooks/Cole.

Luna, G. C. 1991. Street youth: Adaptation and survival in the AIDS decade. *Journal of Adolescent Health* 12(7): 511–514.

Maas, H. S. and R. E. Engler. 1959. *Children in Need of Parents.* New York: Columbia University Press.

Mallon, G. P. 1992a. Gay and no place to go: Assessing the needs of gay and lesbian adolescents in out-of-home care settings. *Child Welfare* 71(6): 547–556.

Mallon, G. P. 1992b. Serving the needs of gay and lesbian adolescents in residential treatment centers. *Residential Treatment for Children and Youth* 10(2): 47–61.

Mallon, G. P. 1994. We don't exactly get the "welcome wagon": The experience of gay and lesbian adolescents in New York City's child welfare system. D.S.W. dissertation, City University of New York.

Mallon, G. P. 1997. Toward a competent child welfare service delivery system for gay and lesbian adolescents and their families. *Journal of Multicultural Social Work* 5(3/4):177–194.

Mallon, G. P. (in press). After care, then where? Evaluating outcomes of an independent living program. *Child Welfare.*

Maluccio, A. N. and E. Fein. 1985. Growing up in foster care. *Children and Youth Services Review* 7: 123–134.

Malyon, A. K. 1981. The homosexual adolescent: Developmental issues and social bias. *Child Welfare League of America* 60(5): 321–330.

Malyon, A. K. 1982. Psychotherapeutic implications of internalized homophobia in gay men. *Journal of Homosexuality,* 7(2/3): 59–69.

Marcia, J. E. 1980. Identity in adolescence. In J. Adelson, ed., *Handbook of Adolescent Psychiatry,* pp. 159–187. New York: Wiley.

Martin, A. D. 1982. Learning to hide: The socialization of the gay adolescent. In S. C. Feinstein, J. G. Looney, A. Schartzberg, and A. Sorosky, eds., *Adolescent Psychiatry: Developmental and Clinical Studies,* vol. 10. Chicago: University of Chicago Press.

Mayer, M. F., L. H. Richman, and E. A. Balcerzak. 1978. *Group Care of Children: Crossroads and Transitions.* New York: Child Welfare League of America.

McCullagh, J. 1995. Accessible child welfare services for lesbian, gay and bisexual youth. *Communicate: The Newspaper of the Children's Aid Society of Metropolitan Toronto* 7(2): 10–11.

McDonald, H. B. and A. I. Steinhorn. 1990. Lesbian and gay youth. In H. B. McDonald and A. I. Steinhorn, eds., *Homosexuality: A Practical Guide to Counseling Gay and Lesbian Parents and Their Families,* pp. 64–76. New York: Continuum.

McGowan, B. and W. Meezan, eds. 1983. *Child Welfare: Current Dilemmas—Future Directions.* Itasca, Ill: F. E. Peacock.

Meston, J. 1988. Preparing young people in Canada for emancipation from child welfare care. *Child Welfare* 67:625–634.

Meyer, C. 1996. Reflection. *Reflections: Narratives of Professional Helping* 2(2): 49–65.

Miles, M. and A. Huberman. 1984. *Qualitative Data Analysis.* Beverly Hills: Sage Publications.

Minton, H. L. and G. J. McDonald. 1984. Homosexual identity formation as a developmental process. In J. P. De Cecco and M. G. Shively, eds., *Origins of Sexuality and Homosexuality,* pp. 91–104. New York: Harrington Park Press.

Miranda, D. 1996. I hated myself. In P. Kay, A. Estepa, and A. Desetta eds., *Out With It: Gay and Straight Teens Write About Homosexuality,* pp. 34–39. New York: Youth Communications.

Mizrahi, T. and J. S. Abramson. 1994. Collaboration between social workers and physicians: A emerging typology. In E. Sherman and W. Reid, eds., *Qualitative Research in Social Work,* pp. 135–151. New York: Columbia University Press.

Monette, P. 1992. *Becoming a Man: Half a Life Story.* New York: Harcourt Brace Jovanovich.

Murphy, G. J. 1981. The institutionalized adolescent and the ethics of desexualization. In D. A. Shore and H. l. Gochros, eds., *Sexual Problems of Adolescents in Institutions*, pp.27–35. Springfield, Ill.: Charles C. Thomas.

Musto, M. and S. Bright. 1993. Gaydar: Using that intuitive sixth sense or, it takes one to know one. *Out* (November): 120- 124.

Newman, B. M. and P. R. Newman. 1987. *Development Through Life: A Psychosocial Approach*. 4th ed. Belmont, Calif.: Dorsey Press.

Newton, D. E. 1978. Homosexual behavior and child molestation: A review of the evidence. *Adolescence* 13(49): 205–215.

O'Brien, C. A., R. Travers, and L. Bell. 1993. *No Safe Bed: Lesbian, Gay, and Bisexual Youth in Residential Services*. Toronto: Central Toronto Youth Services.

Offer, D. and J. B. Offer. 1975. *From Teenage to Young Manhood: A Psychological Study*. New York: Basic Books.

Offer, D., E. Ostrov, and K. Howard. 1981. *The Adolescent: A Psychological Self-Portrait*. New York: Basic Books.

Opie, A. 1992. Qualitative research appropriation of the "other" and empowerment. *Feminist Review* 40: 52–69.

Pecora, P. J., J. K. Whittaker, A. N. Maluccio, R. P. Barth, and R. D. Plotnick. 1992. *The Child Welfare Challenge*. Hawthorne, N.Y.: Aldine de Gruyter.

Pelton, L. H. 1989. *For Reasons of Poverty: A Critical Analysis of the Public Child Welfare System in the United States*. New York: Praeger.

Peplau, L. A. 1991. Lesbian and gay relationships. In J. C. Gonsiorek and J. D. Weinrich, eds., *Homosexuality: Research Implications for Public Policy*, pp. 177–198. Newbury Park, Calif.: Sage Publications.

P-FLAG (Parents and Friends of Lesbians and Gays). 1990. *Why Is My Child Gay?* Washington, D.C.: Parents and Friends of Lesbians and Gays.

Pharr, S. 1988. *Homophobia: A Weapon of Sexism*. Little Rock: Chardon Press.

Polsky, H. 1962. *Cottage Six: The Social System of Delinquent Boys in Residential Treatment*. New York: Russell Sage Foundation.

Raines, J. C. 1990. Empathy in clinical social work. *Clinical Social Work Journal* 18(1): 57–72.

Reid, J. 1973. *The Best Little Boy in the World*. New York: Ballantine Books.

Reid, W. 1994. Reframing the epistemological debate. In E. Sherman and W. Reid, eds., *Qualitative Research in Social Work*, pp. 464–481. New York: Columbia University Press.

Reiter, L. 1991. Developmental origins of antihomosexual prejudice in heterosexual men and women. *Clinical Social Work Journal* 19(2): 163–175.

Remafedi, G. 1987a. Male homosexuality: The adolescent's perspective. *Pediatrics* 79: 326–330.

Remafedi, G. 1987b. Adolescent homosexuality: Psychosocial and implications. *Pediatrics* 79: 331–337.

Remafedi, G., ed. 1994. *The Denial of Death*. Boston: Alyson Publications.

Rich, A. 1983. Compulsory heterosexuality and lesbian existence. In A. Snitow, C. Stansell, and S. Thompson, eds., *Powers of Desire: The Politics of Sexuality*, pp. 177–205. New York: Monthly Review Press.

Ricketts, W. 1991. *Lesbians and Gay Men as Foster Parents*. Portland: University of Southern Maine.

Ricketts, W. and R. A. Achtenberg. 1987. The adoptive and foster gay and lesbian parent. In F. W. Bozett, ed., *Gay and Lesbian Parents*, pp. 89–111. New York: Praeger Press.

Ricketts, W. and R. A. Achtenberg. 1990. Adoption and foster parenting for lesbians and gay men: Creating new traditions in family. *Marriage and Family Review* 14(3/4): 83–118.

Rindfleisch, N. 1993. Combatting institutional abuse. In C. E. Schaefer and A. Swanson, eds., *Children in Residential Care: Critical Issues in Treatment*, pp. 263–283. Northvale, N.J.: Jason Aronson.

Robinson, K. E. 1991. Gay youth support groups: An opportunity for social work intervention. *Social Work* 36(5): 458–459.

Rofes, E. R. 1983. Lesbian and gay youth suicide. In E. R. Rofes, ed., *I Thought People Like That Killed Themselves*, pp. 36–48. San Francisco: Grey Fox Press.

Rofes, E. R. 1996. *Reinventing the Tribe*. New York: Haworth Press.

Rzepnicki, T. L. and T. J. Stein. 1985. Permanency planning for children in foster care: A review of projects. *Children and Youth Services Review* 7: 219–236.

Saperstein, S. 1981. Lesbian and gay adolescents: The need for family support. *Catalyst* 3/4(12): 61–69.

Savin-Williams, R. C. 1994. Verbal and physical abuse as stressors in the lives of lesbian, gay male, and bisexual youths: Associations with school problems, running away, substance abuse, prostitution, suicide. *Journal of Consulting and Clinical Practice* 62: 261–269.

Savin-Williams, R. C. 1995. Lesbian, gay male, and bisexual adolescents. In A. R. D'Augelli and C. J. Patterson, eds., *Lesbian, Gay, and Bisexual Identities Over the Lifespan: Psychological Perspectives*, pp. 165–189. New York; Oxford University Press.

Savin-Williams, R. C. and R. G. Rodriguez. 1993. A developmental clinical perspective on lesbian, gay male, and bisexual youth. In T. P. Gullotta, G. R. Adams, and R. Montemayor, eds., *Adolescent Sexual: Advances in Adolescent Development*, vol. 5, pp. 77–101. Newbury Park, Calif.: Sage Publications.

Schaefer, C. E. 1980. The impact of peer culture in the residential treatment of youth. *Adolescence* 15(60): 831–845.

Schneider, M. 1988. *Often Invisible: Counselling Gay and Lesbian Youth*. Toronto: Toronto Central Youth Services.

Schneider, M. 1989. Sappho was a right-on adolescent. In G. Herdt, ed., *Gay and Lesbian Youth*, pp. 111–130. New York: Haworth Press.

Schneider, M. 1991. Developing services for lesbian and gay adolescents. *Canadian Journal of Community Mental Health* 10(1): 133–151.

Schneider, M. and B. Tremble. 1985. Gay or straight? Working with the confused adolescent. *Journal of Homosexuality* 4(1/2): 71–82.

Schon, D. A. 1995. Reflective inquiry in social work practice. In P. McCartt-Hess and E. J. Mullen, eds., *Practitioner-Researcher Partnerships: Building Knowledge from, in, and for Practice*, pp. 31–55. Washington, D.C.: National Association of Social Workers.

Schorr, L. B. 1988. *Within Our Reach: Breaking the Cycle of Disadvantage*. New York: Doubleday.

Seattle Commission on Children and Youth. 1988. *Report on Gay and Lesbian Youth in Seattle*. Seattle: Seattle Commission on Children and Youth.

Seidel, J. V., R. Kjolseth, and E. Seymour. 1988. *The Ethnograph (Version 3.0): Software for Qualitative Analysis*. Corvaillis, Ore.: Qualis Research Associates.

Shernoff, M. and D. Finnegan. 1991. Family treatment with chemically dependent gay men and lesbians. *Journal of Chemical Dependency* 4(1): 121–135.

Shore, D. A. and H. L. Gochros, eds. 1981. *Sexual Problems of Adolescents in Institutions*. Springfield, Ill.: Charles C. Thomas.

Silverstein, C. 1977. *A Family Matter: A Parent's Guide to Homosexuality*. New York: McGraw Hill.

Simon, B. L. 1987. *Never Married Women*. Philadelphia: Temple University Press.

Simon, B. L. 1994. *The Empowerment Tradition in American Social Work: A History*. New York: Columbia University Press.

Smart, C. 1989. Counseling practice: Counseling homosexual/bisexual people with particular reference to young lesbian women. *International Journal of Adolescence and Youth* 1(4): 379–393.

Soderlind, L. 1992. Rapid growth of gay groups is sign of change. *New York Times*, September 20, p. B3.

Sophie, J. 1985/1986. A critical examination of stage theories of lesbian identity development. *Journal of Homosexuality* 12(3/4): 39–51.

Statistics Canada. 1995. *Children and Families Studies Statistics*. Ottawa: Government of Canada.

Steinhorn, A. 1979. Lesbian adolescents in residential treatment. *Social Casework: The Journal of Contemporary Social Work* 60: 494–498.

Strauss, A. L. and J. Corbin. 1990. *Basics of Qualitative Research: Grounded Theory Procedure and Techniques*. Newbury Park, Calif.: Sage Publications.

Strauss, A. L. and J. Corbin. 1994. Grounded theory methodology: An overview. In N. Denzin and Y. Lincoln, eds. *Handbook of Qualitative Research*, pp. 273–285. Thousand Oaks, Calif.: Sage Publications.

Strommen, E. F. 1989. "You're a what?" Family member reactions to the disclosure of homosexuality. *Journal of Homosexuality* 18(1/2): 37–58.

Sue, D. W. and D. Sue. 1990. *Counseling the Culturally Different*. New York: Wiley.

Sullivan, T. 1994. Obstacles to effective child welfare service with gay and lesbian youths. *Child Welfare* 73(4): 291–304.

Sullivan, T. and M. Schneider. 1987. Development and identity issues in adolescent homosexuality. *Child and Adolescent Social Work* 4(1): 13–24.

Taylor, N. 1994. Gay and lesbian youth: Challenging the policy of denial. In T. De Crescenzo, ed., *Helping Gay and Lesbian Youth: New Policies, New Programs, New Practices*, pp. 39–73. New York: Haworth Press.

Tievsky, D. L. 1988. Homosexual clients and homophobic social workers. *Journal of Independent Social Work* 2(3): 51–62.

Trocme, N., D. McPhee, K. T. Kwok. 1996. Child abuse and neglect in Ontario: Incidence and characteristics. *Child Welfare* 75(3): 563–586.

Troiden, R. R. 1979. Becoming homosexual: A model of gay identity acquisition. *Psychiatry* 42: 362–373.

Troiden, R. R. 1988. *Gay and Lesbian Identity: A Sociological Analysis*. Dix Hills, N.Y.: General Hall.

Troiden, R. R. 1993. The formation of homosexual identities. In L. D. Garnets and D. G. Kimmel, eds., *Psychological Perspectives on Lesbian and Gay Male Experiences*, pp. 191–217. New York: Columbia University Press.

Tuchman, B. W. 1979. In search of history. *Radcliffe Quarterly* 15(1): 33–37.

Tuerk, C. 1995. A son with gentle ways: A therapist-mother's journey. *In ihe Family: A Magazine for Lesbians, Gays, Bisexuals, and Their Relations* (October) 1(1): 18–22.

U.S. House of Representatives. Committee on Ways and Means. 1996. *Green Book*. Washington, D.C.: Government Printing Office.

Valenzuela, W. 1996. A school where I can be myself. In P. Kay, A. Estepa, and A. Desetta, eds., *Out With It: Gay and Straight Teens Write About Homosexuality*, pp. 45–46. New York: Youth Communications.

Vergara, T. L. 1984. Meeting the needs of sexual minority youth: One program's response. *Journal of Social Work and Human Sexuality* 2(2/3): 19–38.

Victim Services/Traveler's Aid. 1991. *Streetwork Project Study*. New York: Victim Services.

Wadley, C. 1996a. Shunned, insulted, threatened. In P. Kay, A. Estepa, and A. Desetta, eds. *Out With It: Gay and Straight Teens Write About Homosexuality*, pp. 57–60. New York: Youth Communications.

Wadley, C. 1996b. Kicked out because she was a lesbian. In P. Kay, A. Estepa, and A. Desetta, eds., *Out With It: Gay and Straight Teens Write About Homosexuality*, pp. 58–60. New York: Youth Communications.

Webber, M. 1991. *Street Kids: The Tragedy of Canada's Runaways*. Toronto: University of Toronto Press.

Weick, A. 1990. Overturning oppressions: An analysis of empancipatory change. Presentation at the University of Kansas symposium "Building on Women's

Strengths: A Social Work Agenda for the Twenty-First Century, Lawrence, Kansas.

Whitlock, K. 1989. *Bridges of Respect*. Philadelphia: American Friends Service Committee.

Whittaker, J. 1981. Family involvement in residential child care: A support system for biological parents. In A. N. Maluccio and P. Sinanoglu, eds., *The Challenge of Partnership: Working with Parents in Foster Care,* pp. 67–89. New York: Child Welfare League of America.

Whittaker, J. 1985. Group and institutional care: An overview. In J. Laird and A. Hartman, eds., *A Handbook of Child Welfare: Context, Knowledge, and Practice* pp. 617–637. New York: Free Press.

Williams, W. L. 1992. *The Spirit and the Flesh: Sexual Diversity in American Indian Culture*. Boston: Beacon Press.

Wisniewski, J. J. and B. G. Toomey. 1987. Are social workers homophobic? *Social Work* 32(5): 454–455.

Wolin, S. J. and S. Wolin. 1994. *The Resilient Self: How Survivors of Troubled Families Rise Above Adversity*. New York: Villard Books.

Zide, M. R. and A. L. Cherry. 1992. A typology of runaway youths: An empirically based definition. *Child and Adolescent Social Work* 9(2): 155–168.

Index